SMART CHICKEN

D0719734

Also by Jane Kinderlehrer

CONFESSIONS OF A SNEAKY ORGANIC COOK

HOW TO FEEL YOUNGER LONGER

THE ART OF COOKING WITH LOVE AND WHEAT GERM

COOKING KOSHER THE NATURAL WAY

SMART COOKIES

SMART MUFFINS

SMART BREAKFASTS

SMART CHICKEN

---

101 Tasty and Healthy Poultry Dishes, Plus Stuffings and Accompaniments

---

JANE KINDERLEHRER

Illustrations by Carol Inouye

NEWMARKET PRESS

New York

THE NEWMARKET JANE KINDERLEHRER SMART FOOD SERIES

Copyright © 1991 by Jane Kinderlehrer
Illustrations copyright © 1991 by Carol Inouye

This book is published simultaneously
in the United States of America and in Canada.

All rights reserved.
This book may not be reproduced,
in whole or in part, in any form, without permission.
Inquiries should be addressed to:
Permissions Dept., Newmarket Press, 18 East 48th Street,
New York, New York 10017.

First Edition

91 92 93 94   10 9 8 7 6 5 4 3 2 1 PB
91 92 93 94   10 9 8 7 6 5 4 3 2 1 HC

Library of Congress Cataloging-in-Publication Data

Kinderlehrer, Jane.
    Smart chicken : 101 tasty and healthy poultry dishes, plus stuffings
and accompaniments / Jane Kinderlehrer.
        p.   cm. — (The Newmarket Jane Kinderlehrer smart food series)
Includes index.
ISBN 1-55704-073-7 (paperback)
ISBN 1-55704-100-8 (hardcover)
1. Cookery (chicken) I. Title. II. Series.
TX750.5.C45K56   1991
641.6'65—dc20   90-27453
                                                                    CIP

Quantity Purchases

Companies, professional groups, clubs, and other organizations may qualify for special terms when ordering quantities of this title. For information, contact: Special Sales Dept., Newmarket Press, 18 East 48th Street, New York, New York 10017, or call (212) 832-3575.

Book design by Ruth Kolbert
Manufactured in the United States

*Dedicated to my sister, Betty Kane,
and my brother, Harry Arden,
in nostalgic recollection of the many chicken dinners
we have so happily shared*

———————————

Contents

METRIC CONVERSION CHART

1 teaspoon = 5 ml.   1 tablespoon = 15 ml.
1 ounce = 30 ml.   1 cup = 240 ml./.24 l.
1 quart = 950 ml./.95 l.   1 gallon = 3.80 l.

1 ounce = 28 gr.   1 pound = 454 gr./.454 kg.

F°	200	225	250	275	300	325	350	375	400	425	450
C°	93	107	121	135	149	163	177	191	204	218	232

ABBREVIATIONS

cal = calories   sat = saturated
pro = protein   unsat = unsaturated
g = gram   chol = cholesterol
mg = milligram   tr = trace

INTRODUCTION

Chicken Every
Sunday, Monday, Tuesday . . .

Remember when "chicken in every pot" and "chicken every Sunday" were the hallmarks of "prosperity"? That was long ago, when chicken, because of its succulent goodness, was everybody's favorite special-occasion meal.

It still is. But because of our current concern over the danger of cholesterol-raising saturated fats, chicken and its cousins in the fowl family have won new prestige and a favored spot on the menu.

Chicken is a smart choice not just for special occasions but also for every day of the week. Poultry is less costly, less fatty, and higher in nutritional value in proportion to calories than either beef or lamb. And though chicken's succulence makes it taste like a zillion calories, it's actually a great food to lose weight on while enjoying the pleasures of the palate.

The usual portion of 3½ ounces of chicken or turkey provides only 150 calories (slightly more for dark meat), plus an impressive 28 to 31 grams of protein (about half the usual adult daily requirement), as well as potassium, iron, phosphorus, and calcium. Chicken also contains vitamin A. Both chicken and turkey have some B vitamins, with a significant content of the cholesterol-lowering B vitamin niacin.

And with 101 quick and easy "smart" recipes to choose from, chicken three times a week or even every day need never be boring. On the contrary, you'll find that your chicken dinners with their heavenly cooking aromas will enhance your family's joy of eating.

Ounce for ounce, chicken contains as much protein as red meat, but with far less fat. And the fat in chicken is not the cholesterol-raising saturated type. Far from it! The fat in chicken is predominantly heart-healthy monounsaturated, which means that chicken skin is not the cholesterol-raising villain many people believe it to be. Chicken skin is only 17 percent fat and, when rendered, can add the most delectable of flavors and irresistible crunch to some of my favorite dishes, such as chopped liver and potato knishes. (See Index listing for specific recipes.)

Chicken is so versatile, there's something about it to please everyone at the table, even the picky eater. There's dark and white meat; there are drumsticks, wings, thighs, and breasts, each with a unique flavor and texture.

However, not all chicken dinners are smart.

A chicken dinner is smart when it is low in fat, low in sodium, low in calories, and served with high-fiber accompaniments.

For instance, a 3½-ounce serving of processed chicken nuggets can contain as much as 323 calories, 20 grams of fat, and 512 milligrams of sodium. A boneless chicken breast that is steamed, baked, or sautéed contains just 173 calories, 4½ grams of fat, and 77 milligrams of sodium.

The uses of chicken are countless. Its succulence can be part of every meal except dessert.

As the nineteenth-century French gastronome Jean Anthelme Brillat-Savarin wrote, "Poultry is for the cook what canvas is to the painter. It is served to us boiled, roasted, fried, hot or cold, whole or in pieces, with or without sauce, boned, skinned, stuffed, and always with equal success."

With this book as your guide, you can perfect your technique with all these methods, prepare a variety of delectable meals with ease and pizzazz, and make them all smart.

MEET THE MEMBERS OF THE POULTRY FAMILY

Cornish hens. Also called Rock Cornish hens. A young, small chicken that weighs ¾ to 1½ pounds—tender, juicy meat—great for roasting and also very tasty braised, broiled, or fried.

Broilers. The terms "broiler" and "fryer" are frequently used interchangeably, but a broiler may weigh a little less than a fryer—about 2 to 3 pounds—and is often sold as a "split."

Fryers. Slightly larger than broilers, weighing 3 to 4 pounds, and sometimes called broiler-fryers. They're sold whole, quartered, or cut into serving pieces.

Pullets. Small roasters—4 to 5 pounds—designated mostly for the roasting or stewing pan.

Roasters. Larger chickens, usually served whole—now available in 5- to 7-pound sizes. They carve nicely. Roaster parts are also marketed separately.

Stewing chickens. Older, larger, and tougher but richer in flavor. Weighing about 6 pounds, they're great for soups, stewing, fricassee, or chicken pot pie.

Capons. Very flavorful, tender, and juicy, these large and meaty castrated roosters may weigh 6 to 12 pounds. Superb for roasting.

Duck—broiler-fryer. Very young (under 8 weeks old), less than 3 pounds, excellent fried or broiled.

Duck—roaster. Eight to 16 weeks old, fatty and tender—best roasted or braised.

Goose. All meat is dark and fatty. When 4 to 12 pounds, it is best roasted. When over 12 pounds, it's best braised.

Squab. Domesticated pigeon weighing less than 1 pound. Excellent roasted or braised.

Turkey—fryer-roaster. Small (4 to 9 pounds), young, and tender, with smooth skin and flexible breastbone; excellent broiled, oven-fried, or roasted.

Turkey—young. Usually 7 to 15 pounds, best when roasted.

Turkey—yearling. Twenty to 30 pounds, usually roasted or braised.

SMART TIPS FOR CLEVER COOKS

Most recipes for the preparation of poultry call for added fat in the stuffing and on the bird. The new dietary guidelines state that no more than 30 percent of the calories should be derived from fat. Many physicians are advising no more than 20 percent as a preventative measure and no more than 15 percent as a therapeutic measure for those who already have cardiovascular problems.

To skin or not to skin: Does removing the skin before cooking chicken cut down on fat? No, according to researchers from the University of Minnesota. They found that it doesn't matter much whether you remove the skin before or after cooking. Even though about half the fat in poultry comes from the skin, apparently no significant amount is transferred to the meat during cooking. Skinning poultry before cooking only leads to drier—not leaner—meat, the researchers found.

Here are some tips to help you reduce the fat and savor the flavor:

- Cut away the visible fat and extra skin from chicken and other poultry before cooking, but do not discard it. Render it. (See the recipe for chicken fat.) Use the rendered chicken fat (schmaltz) to enhance the flavor of many poultry dishes. Chicken fat is a far better cooking fat than butter if you're concerned about cholesterol.
- Sauté onions for the poultry dressing without fat. Here's how: Use a tiny bit of water, just enough to barely cover the bottom of a large pan. Add onions and turn up the heat. When water begins to boil, cover the pan with a tight-fitting lid and lower the heat to medium for about 10 to 15 minutes. The onions will be nicely sautéed and sweet-tasting. Or microwave the onions

with a little water or chicken broth, but without fat, for about 2 minutes on high.

- Follow the same procedure for garlic and julienned vegetables.
- To make a sauce that needs a glaze, remove the onions when they are ready. Take a teaspoon of arrowroot powder or corn-starch and dissolve with a teaspoon of water. Stir until thick-ened. Add spices, herbs, and juices to flavor the sauce.
- To sauté chicken or turkey without fat, place in a sauté pan with 2 ice cubes and stir constantly to prevent sticking.
- Sauté thinly sliced vegetables such as yellow squash, zucchini, peppers, and onions in 2 tablespoons of tomato juice. Toss with herbs such as thyme, basil, and oregano and serve as a side dish. A delicious source of fiber.
- Save the renderings in the bottom of the broiler or roaster pan to make a natural gravy without added fat. To degrease the renderings quickly, place them in a measuring cup. Then sub-merge the cup in ice water three-quarters of the way up. The fat will rise to the top and begin to thicken, allowing you to skim it off easily. Or place the bowl of drippings in the freezer for 10 minutes, then skim off the hardened fat that rises to the surface. Reheat the remaining juices, and season with herbs and spices to taste.
- To thicken gravy, first skim off excess fat from the pan drip-pings. Combine 2 tablespoons of flour with 1 cup of water or stock, and blend in a screw-top jar or in a blender or food processor. Add the flour mixture to the pan drippings and stir constantly over medium heat until thickened.
- When you're reheating meat, keep it moist and flavorful with-out adding fat. Place a lettuce leaf in the bottom of a casserole or pie plate, then place the meat on the lettuce and cover with another lettuce leaf. Add a tiny bit of water or broth to the

bottom of the pan and heat at 350 degrees until the meat is heated through.

• Many recipes call for fats to thicken a soup base. Instead, try boiling potatoes, puréeing them, and using this purée as a thickener. Other puréed vegetables can also be used, not only as thickeners but also as flavor and nutrient enhancers.

HELPFUL HINTS

• To freeze fresh poultry, remove the store wrapping and rinse the poultry in cold water. Pat dry with paper towels, then wrap in freezer paper, heavy-duty foil, or plastic wrap. Label each package, noting the date, which parts are included, how many pieces, and where it is placed in the freezer. It will keep up to 6 months.

• Hard-frozen poultry can go right from the store into your freezer without rewrapping. Do not allow it to thaw at all.

• If it has thawed in the store or in getting it home, cook it promptly and then freeze it or use it.

• Never refreeze thawed, uncooked chicken.

• If you're making a stew, chicken can go right into the pot from the freezer.

• If you're using it for fried, broiled, barbecued, or roasted dishes, thaw it first. It will cook more evenly.

• If a recipe calls for bread crumbs, remember that one standard-size slice of bread will yield ½ to ¾ cup of fresh bread crumbs. That same slice of bread when dried will yield about 3 to 4 tablespoons of dried bread crumbs. Use about half the amount of dried crumbs as a replacement for fresh crumbs.

- To broil chicken successfully, place the chicken on the rack of broiler pan and broil 4 to 7 inches from heat, turning and basting frequently until chicken is tender, usually in about 40 minutes. To glaze, brush chicken with the glaze during the last 20 minutes.
- When a recipe calls for pounding chicken cutlets to flatten them to a uniform thickness, place the cutlets between two sheets of waxed paper and pound with the bottom of a skillet.
- When a recipe calls for sautéeing onions with fat, you can eliminate the fat by using a little chicken or vegetable broth, or by using the microwave on full power for about 2 minutes for 3 tablespoons of chopped onions, covered.
- Many recipes call for herbal seasoning. This is available commercially (for example, Mrs. Dash, Herbal Bouquet, or Spike) or you can make your own and use it in place of salt.

Herbal Seasoning

$\frac{1}{8}$ teaspoon cayenne powder
$\frac{1}{4}$ teaspoon garlic powder
1 tablespoon dried parsley
$\frac{1}{2}$ teaspoon paprika

$\frac{1}{2}$ teaspoon dried thyme
$\frac{1}{2}$ teaspoon dried marjoram
$\frac{1}{2}$ teaspoon onion powder
1 teaspoon roasted sesame seeds

Crush or blend in a seed mill or blender until powdery. Place in a shaker topped jar.

1
CHICKEN SALADS

Tropical Chicken Salad
Waldorf Chicken Salad
Chicken Pasta Salad
Quickie Chicken Salad—Italian Style

For lunch, brunch, a buffet spread, or a take-along dish for a special occasion, chicken salad is a popular choice. It's the perfect way to use leftover chicken or turkey without subjecting its nutrients to more heat.

Go creative with your poultry salads. Vary the flavor and texture of your salads with crunchy almonds, walnuts, peanuts, or hazelnuts. Add to their succulence with grapes, peaches, pineapple, apples, raisins, or currants. Make it tantalizing with a touch of raspberry or balsamic vinegar in a piquant salad dressing. Stuff it in avocados or in red, yellow, or green peppers. Serve a small portion as a prelude to a sumptuous meal or a larger portion as an elegant, satisfying meal in itself.

Tropical Chicken Salad

A lovely medley of fruits and nuts makes this salad a melody of delightful flavors and textures.

2 cups cooked chicken, cut in bite-size pieces
1 cup diced celery
1 20-ounce can pineapple chunks, drained (retain juice)
2 oranges, peeled and sectioned
½ cup chopped pecans, lightly roasted

1 cup seedless grapes
4 tablespoons reduced-calorie mayonnaise combined with 4 tablespoons of the retained pineapple juice
romaine lettuce leaves

Combine all ingredients except lettuce in a glass serving bowl. Serve on the lettuce leaves.

Yield: 6 servings.

Each serving provides: 220 cal, 16 g pro, 1.2 g sat fat, 7.2 g unsat fat, 46 mg chol.

Waldorf Chicken Salad

This perennial favorite, moistened with tofu mayonnaise, features tart apples and sweet grapes—a very tasty combo that provides both vitamin C and fiber.

2 cups cooked chicken, cut in bite-size pieces
1 large Granny Smith apple, unpeeled
2 stalks celery, sliced diagonally
1 small green or red pepper, diced
½ small onion, diced
1 cup seedless red or green grapes, cut in halves

½ cup walnuts, coarsely chopped
1 cup raisins
⅔ cup orange juice
½ cup soft tofu or plain yogurt
⅛ teaspoon ground nutmeg (optional)
dark green lettuce leaves

In a glass bowl, combine the chicken, apple, celery, pepper, onion, grapes, and half of the walnuts.

In a small bowl, beat with a fork the orange juice, yogurt or tofu, and nutmeg until well blended. Pour over the chicken mixture and mix well. Garnish with the remaining walnuts. Serve on the lettuce leaves. **Yield:** 4 servings.

Each serving provides: 330 cal, 28 g pro, 1 g sat fat, 11.5 g unsat fat, 46 mg chol.

Chicken Pasta Salad

Pasta with its complex carbohydrates marries very well with high-protein chicken, making this salad a satisfying, nutritious meal in itself. Delightful served on the patio when warm breezes are blowing.

¼ cup reduced-calorie
   mayonnaise or salad
   dressing
2 tablespoons chicken broth
½ teaspoon dried crushed
   thyme
½ teaspoon dill weed
1 teaspoon Dijon mustard
1 teaspoon herbal seasoning
2 cups cooked chicken, cut
   in bite-size chunks

1 cup corkscrew noodles,
   cooked and drained
   (about 2 cups cooked)
2 tablespoons oat bran
2 scallions, chopped
1 cup chopped tomato
1 cup green pepper, cut in
   chunks
   dark green lettuce leaves

Combine the salad dressing, chicken broth, thyme, dill, mustard, and herbal seasoning. Mix well. Add the remaining ingredients except the lettuce leaves. Mix to combine the ingredients. Chill several hours before serving. Serve on the lettuce leaves.

Yield: 4 servings.

Each serving provides: 227 cal, 24 g pro, 1 g sat fat, 2 g unsat fat, 46 mg chol.

Quickie Chicken Salad—Italian Style

A very popular, easy-to-assemble salad; great for a casual brunch or buffet.

3 cups cooked chicken, cut
    in bite-size chunks
1 cup chopped celery
1 (6-ounce) jar marinated
    artichoke hearts,
    drained
½ cup pitted ripe olives,
    drained and sliced

1 can (8 ounce) water
    chestnuts, drained and
    sliced
½ cup Italian dressing
    dark green lettuce leaves
    tomato wedges

Combine all the ingredients except the lettuce leaves and tomato wedges. Chill. Serve in a bowl lined with the lettuce leaves. Garnish with the tomato wedges.

Yield: 6 servings.

Each serving provides: 174 cal, 28 g pro, 11 g unsat fat, 50 mg chol.

2
ROAST CHICKEN

Roast Chicken with Lemon and Wine
Roast Chicken with Garlic, Apples, and Rutabagas
Roast Capon with Onions and Prunes
Roast Chicken with Sweet Pepper Chutney
Roast Chicken with Rosemary and Garlic

Nothin' says lovin' like a roast chicken in the oven. I like to bring the roast chicken to the table in all its glory—uncut and majestic in its crisp brown overcoat. There's nothing like this presentation to get the salivary juices flowing.

Roasting is an easy and tasty way of preparing all kinds of young, tender poultry—chicken, game hen, turkey, duck, and goose.

First, to truss, pull the skin flaps over the body and neck cavities, and either sew the skin in place or use skewers. Tie the legs together, then fold the wings back and under the bird, and tie them close to the body.

Place whole poultry breast side up on a rack in a shallow pan. Roast at 325 to 350 degrees. Baste every 30 to 45 minutes. About 30 minutes before the bird is completely roasted, untie the trussed legs to facilitate browning of the under side of the legs.

Roast chickens can be simple or exotic accompanied or stuffed with fruits, vegetables, grains, or nuts. Approach the roasting of the bird with a creative gleam and a shelf full of herbs and spices.

Choose a large roaster or capon for 6 or more diners, and figure 15 to 20 minutes per pound in a 350-degree oven. Smaller chickens need about 25 minutes per pound.

To determine if the bird is ready for its grand entrance, pierce the thickest part of the thigh with a fork. The juices should be clear, without a trace of pink or red.

STUFFING THE BIRD

To stuff or not to stuff? That is the question. Is it better to pile this tasty mixture into the body cavity, or to bake it separately? Remember that there is a symbiotic relationship between the bird and the stuffing. Each contributes moisture and flavor to the other. If you opt for stuffing the bird, consider this new method, which makes for a fantastic presentation and keeps even the usually dry breast meat moist, tender, and flavorful, transforming a humdrum stuffed bird into elegant gourmet fare. The key is to insert the stuffing between the flesh and the skin.

Here's how: Slip your fingers between skin and flesh, starting at the neck. Work your way down, loosening the flesh over each breast, and then free the skin from the legs, leaving the skin attached at the very tips of the drumsticks.

Starting at the neck, push the filling under the skin with one hand and use the other hand on the outside of the bird to mold the stuffing into place. Stuff the drumsticks and thighs, then make a thick coating over the breasts. This will protect the breast meat from drying out. Then tuck the neck flap over the opening and tuck it securely under the bird. Place the bird in a roasting pan and then in a hot oven (about 400 degrees). After 10 minutes, lower the heat to 350 degrees. After about 30 minutes, baste frequently with the pan juices.

How much stuffing do you need? Figure 2 cups for a 4-pound chicken. Stuffing can be prepared and refrigerated a day ahead, but never stuff the bird until you are ready to put it in the oven. To be prepared for the usual enthusiasm for "more stuffing, please," it's a good idea to prepare extra stuffing and bake it in a casserole for about an hour along with the chicken.

Roast Chicken
with Lemon and Wine

My family's favorite chicken recipe. It's simple, quick, moist, tender, and full of flavor. Serve with a tossed salad and sweet potato-apple-granola casserole.

1 whole chicken, about 3½
    pounds
juice of 1 lemon
1 clove garlic, crushed
½ teaspoon ground ginger
½ teaspoon dry mustard

¼ teaspoon crushed dry
    thyme
¼ teaspoon dried sage
1 teaspoon paprika
½ cup dry white wine

Preheat oven to 350°F.

Clean the chicken and pat it dry.

Sprinkle with the lemon juice and rub with the crushed garlic inside and out. Combine the spices in a shaker-top jar and sprinkle the mixture over the chicken, coating all surfaces.

Tie the legs together and place the chicken breast side up in the roasting pan. Add the wine.

Bake for 1¼ hours or until the juices run clear.

Yield: 4 servings.

Each serving provides: 244 cal, 42 g pro, 2 g sat fat, 5 g unsat fat, 157 mg chol, 146 mg sodium.

Roast Chicken with Garlic, Apples, and Rutabagas

The apples, garlic, and rutabagas are roasted with the chicken, then mashed and served as a lovely, tasty accompaniment.

1 roasting chicken, about 3 pounds
2 teaspoons paprika
½ teaspoon freshly ground pepper
½ teaspoon ground ginger
½ teaspoon dry mustard
1 teaspoon chicken fat or olive oil

3 medium-size apples, unpeeled, cored, and cut into eighths
1 large rutabaga, peeled and thinly sliced
4 cloves garlic, peeled
3 tablespoons lemon juice

Preheat oven to 325°F.

Combine the paprika, pepper, ginger, and mustard, and rub the chicken with them, inside and out.

Place the chicken in a roasting pan. Arrange the apples, rutabagas, and garlic around the chicken, then sprinkle the lemon juice over all.

Roast until golden brown, about 1¼ hours. Baste several times with the pan juices.

When the juices run clear, remove the chicken to a serving platter. Skim the fat from the roasting pan, then mash the apples, rutabagas, and garlic together with the pan juices. Serve with the chicken in a separate bowl.

Yield: 4 servings.

Each serving provides: 370 cal, 40 g pro, 4 g sat fat, 13 g unsat fat, 80 mg chol, 190 mg sodium.

Roast Capon with Onions and Prunes

Capons are more meaty, more tender, and more flavorful than roasters. They are also more fatty. The accompanying onions and prunes are an excellent accompaniment, providing fiber and nutrients that help in the utilization of fats.

1 9- to 10-pound capon
   herbal seasoning and
     freshly ground pepper
      to taste
1 teaspoon paprika

1 clove garlic
½ pound seedless prunes
2 medium-size onions,
     peeled
2 cups water

Preheat oven to 425°F.

Soak the prunes in the water.

Rub the capon with the garlic, and sprinkle inside and out with the seasonings.

Place the capon on its side in a shallow roasting pan and scatter the onions, gizzard, and neck around it.

Roast for 20 minutes and turn the capon on its other side.

Roast the capon, basting frequently 20 minutes longer, and turn the bird on its back.

Roast, basting, for another 20 minutes.

Reduce the oven heat to 350°F. Add the prunes. Cover the breast of the capon with foil, and continue roasting and basting for 30 minutes longer.

Pour off the fat from the roasting pan, and place the pan on the stove. Add the water in which the prunes were soaked, and stir with a wooden spoon to dissolve the brown particles that cling to the bottom and sides of the pan. Serve the capon carved, with the prunes and pan gravy.

Yield: About 10 servings.

Each serving provides: 355 cal, 34 g pro, 4 g sat fat, 11 g unsat fat, 66 mg chol, 265 mg sodium.

Roast Chicken with Sweet Pepper Chutney

The chutney adds a zesty, piquant flavor and may be made ahead of time and stored in the refrigerator for up to 2 weeks.

1 *broiler-fryer, about 3 pounds*
2 *cloves garlic, peeled and crushed*
 herbal seasoning and freshly grated pepper to taste
1 *tablespoon chicken fat or olive oil*
1 *medium yellow onion, sliced (about 1 cup)*
1 *large red bell pepper, seeded and cut into chunks (about 1¼ cups)*

½ *teaspoon red pepper flakes*
¼ *teaspoon ground cloves*
½ *cup raisins*
1 *cup whole peeled tomatoes, drained*
2 *tablespoons honey*
2 *tablespoons lemon juice*
1 *teaspoon grated lemon rind*

Preheat oven to 450°F.

Rub the chicken inside and out with the garlic and the seasonings.

Arrange the chicken on a rack in a shallow baking pan. Roast for 10 minutes. Reduce the oven temperature to 350°F. Roast for 30 minutes, basting with pan juices.

Meanwhile, prepare the chutney.

In a skillet or heavy-bottom saucepan, combine the oil, onion, grated pepper, pepper flakes, and cloves. Cook over medium heat, stirring occasionally until the onions are transparent and the bell pepper is wilted. Add the raisins, tomatoes, honey, lemon juice, and rind. Simmer, uncovered, for about 10 minutes. Remove from the heat and allow to cool.

Serve the chicken either warm or cool, accompanied with the chutney at room temperature.

Yield: 4 servings.

Each serving provides: 150 cal, 25 g pro, 1.5 g sat fat, 2.7 g unsat fat, 66 mg chol.

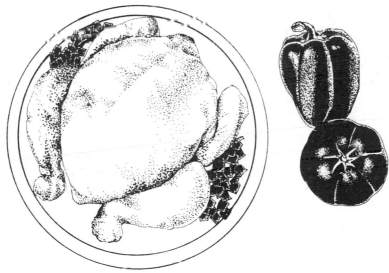

Roast Chicken with Rosemary and Garlic

The marvelous aroma of rosemary and garlic piques the appetite. I like to serve this flavorful chicken with a big tossed salad and julienned carrots steamed with currants.

1 broiler-fryer, 3 to 3½
   pounds
vegetable seasoner and
   pepper to taste
2 sprigs fresh rosemary or ½
   teaspoon dried

2 cloves garlic, unpeeled
1 onion, peeled
¾ cup water

Preheat the oven to 425°F.

Sprinkle the chicken inside and out with the seasonings, then stuff it with the garlic and the rosemary.

Place the chicken on its side in a shallow roaster. Scatter the onion, neck, and gizzards around the chicken. Roast for 15 minutes, then turn the chicken on the other side and continue roasting, basting often for another 15 minutes. Then turn the chicken on its back and continue roasting and basting for 15 minutes.

Pour off the fat from the roasting pan. Add the water, and return the chicken to the oven. Roast 10 minutes longer, basting frequently. Remove from the oven and let stand 10 minutes before carving. Serve with the pan liquid.

Yield: 4 servings.

Each serving provides: 150 cal, 25 g pro, 1.5 g sat fat, 2.7 g unsat fat, 66 mg chol.

3

EXOTIC CHICKEN BREASTS

Chicken with Linguine
Chicken au Poivre
Chicken Almond Delight
Chicken with Pine Nuts
Breast of Chicken Cock-a-doodle-doo
Raisin and Rum Chicken in Creamy Almond Sauce

The breast is especially delectable to lovers of the white meat. It is certainly the most versatile portion of the chicken's anatomy. It can be deboned and stuffed with nuts, seeds, fruits, grains, or vegetables. It can be spread with almond butter, peanut butter, cashew butter, or tahini, but not with dairy butter, which is a saturated fat. Nut butters provide healthier polyunsaturated fats.

Fat of some kind is usually added to chicken breasts because they tend to be dry. Many chefs remove the skin because it is fatty, then add another fat. I prefer to use the fat that is indigenous to the source. I leave the skin on. The fat in the chicken skin not only makes for a deliciously moist and flavorful chicken dish but also one that is much kinder to your heart. The fat in chicken skin is mainly monounsaturated, the kind that tends to lower harmful cholesterol levels. It is not necessary to eat the skin. Just cook with it and limit the addition of other fats.

In recipes that call for cutting up the breast, however, it may be necessary to remove the skin along with the bones. In that case, reserve both the skin and bones to make a tasty stock.

Chicken with Linguine

Savory, satisfying, ready in no time, and high in energetic complex carbohydrates. The added vegetables contribute vitamin B's, carotene, and important antioxidants.

2 whole chicken breasts
2 tablespoons soy sauce
2 tablespoons dry sherry
2 teaspoons cornstarch or
    potato starch
1 8-ounce package linguine,
    cooked
2 tablespoons olive oil or
    chicken fat
1 cup sliced mushrooms

1 cup pea pods or 1 cup
    mung bean sprouts
2 green onions, cut into
    2-inch pieces
1 red pepper, thinly sliced
½ cup chicken broth or ½
    cup water mixed with
    ½ teaspoon chicken-
    flavored bouillon

On a cutting board or double thickness of wax paper, cut each chicken breast in half. Place the pieces skin side up. Work with one half at a time. Using the tip of a sharp knife, start close to the large end of the rib and remove the bones. Slide the skin off. Reserve both skin and bones for stock.

Slice across the width of each half into ½-inch slices.

In a bowl, combine the sliced chicken, soy sauce, sherry, and cornstarch or potato starch.

In a large skillet or wok, heat the oil or chicken fat. Add the mushrooms, pea pods or mung bean sprouts, green onions, and red pepper. Stir quickly until just tender, about 3 minutes. With a slotted spoon, remove the vegetables to a bowl. In the drippings remaining in the skillet or wok, cook the chicken mixture, stirring frequently until the chicken is tender, about 3 minutes. Return the vegetables to the skillet or wok. Add the chicken broth or water and bouillon. Heat to boiling, stirring to loosen the flavorful brown bits from the bottom of the skillet. Add the cooked linguine. Heat the mixture through. Toss to mix well.

Yield: 6 servings.

Each serving provides: 199 cal, 12.7 g pro, 2.3 g sat fat, 6.2 g unsat fat, 74 mg chol.

Chicken au Poivre

Peps up the palate and the conversation. The vegetables round out the nutritional power and contribute beneficial fiber.

4 large whole chicken breasts, boned and split
2 teaspoons coarsely ground black pepper
1 teaspoon herbal seasoning
2 tablespoons olive oil
2 tablespoons chicken fat
1 cup thinly sliced onions
1 cup thinly sliced carrots
1 clove garlic, crushed
2 tablespoons whole wheat flour
½ teaspoon dried thyme
1 bay leaf
3 tablespoons finely chopped fresh parsley
½ cup coarsely chopped celery
½ cup finely chopped leeks or scallions
1 cup dry vermouth
1 cup chicken broth
1 tablespoon prepared mustard, preferably Dijon
1 tablespoon chopped chives

Sprinkle the chicken pieces with the pepper and herbal seasoning.

Heat the oil and chicken fat in a large skillet. Add the onions, carrots, and garlic and cook, stirring, about 10 minutes. Do not allow it to brown. Sprinkle with the flour, and stir to blend. Arrange the chicken pieces, boned-side down, in the skillet and sprinkle with the thyme, bay leaf, parsley, celery, and leeks or scallions. Cover closely and cook for 5 minutes.

Add the vermouth and broth, and cover. Simmer for 20 minutes.

Remove the chicken pieces to a platter and keep warm. Spoon and scrape the sauce into the container of a food processor or blender and blend to a fine purée. Return the sauce to a saucepan and gently heat. Add the mustard, stirring, and remove from the heat. Sprinkle with the chives, and pour the sauce over the chicken. Serve hot.

Yield: 8 servings.

Each serving provides: 203.5 cal, 27 g pro, 3 g sat fat, 8 g unsat fat, 74 mg chol.

Chicken Almond Delight

The intriguing scent and taste of almonds bring a subtle elegance to this very popular dish.

2 chicken breasts, split and boned
4 tablespoons chunky almond butter
½ teaspoon dried thyme
1 cup bread crumbs made from toasted whole wheat pita

2 tablespoons olive oil
1 tablespoon chicken fat
1 clove garlic
½ cup sherry

Pound the breasts flat and spread the almond butter on each. Combine the pita crumbs and thyme. Sprinkle this mixture over the chicken. In a large skillet, heat the oil and chicken fat and sauté the garlic briefly.

Roll up each chicken breast, and anchor with toothpicks. Place them in the skillet, and sauté for 1 minute. Place in a baking dish sprayed with nonstick spray, and bake at 350°F. for 20 minutes. Pour the sherry in the sauté pan, heat, and pour over the chicken breasts.
Yield: 4 servings.

Each serving provides: 381 cal, 24 g pro, 3.8 g sat fat, 16 g unsat fat, 74 mg chol.

Variation 1: Substitute cashew or peanut butter for the almond butter.

Variation 2: For those who are allergic to wheat, substitute crushed rice cakes for the whole wheat pita.

Chicken with Pine Nuts

Lightly roasted pine nuts bring a lovely sensuous flavor to this easily prepared, delightful dish. Pine nuts are a good source of vitamin B complex, vitamin A, and many minerals, and are low in fat. They are expensive, but once in a while they're worth it.

1 tablespoon olive oil
1 tablespoon chicken fat
2 whole chicken breasts,
    deboned and cut in
    2-inch pieces
6 scallions, sliced

2 cloves garlic, minced
2 tomatoes, skinned and
    chopped
½ cup pine nuts, lightly
    roasted

In a large skillet, heat the oil and chicken fat. Over medium heat, cook the chicken until lightly browned. Add the scallions and garlic and cook another minute. Add the tomatoes. Cook for 15 to 20 minutes, or until the chicken is tender and thoroughly cooked. Sprinkle with the pine nuts.

Yield: 4 servings.

Each portion provides: 242 cal, 24 g pro, 2.5 g sat fat, 7 g unsat fat, 74 mg chol.

Breast of Chicken
Cock-a-doodle-doo

So called because of the way it remains moist and tender and puffs up with pride. Serve with sweet potato puff and cranberry chutney.

2 *whole chicken breasts, boned and divided in halves*
¼ *cup whole wheat flour*
3 *tablespoons sesame seeds (optional)*

1 *tablespoon olive or canola oil*
1 *tablespoon chicken fat*

Use the skin and bones to make a flavorful stock, which will be used in the gravy.

Dust the breasts lightly with the flour mixed with the sesame seeds.

Heat the oil and chicken fat together in a heavy skillet. Place the chicken pieces in the hot fat. Shake the pan constantly so the floury crusts do not brown. Cover and cook over very low heat for 10 to 15 minutes, depending on the thickness of the chicken, turning the meat occasionally.

Remove the pan from the heat and allow to stand, covered, about 10 minutes more. The breast will puff up and be unbelievably moist and tender. Remove the chicken from the pan and keep warm.

To make the gravy: Pour off and reserve the fat from the pan. In a saucepan heat 2 tablespoons of the fat and 2 tablespoons of the whole wheat flour. Slowly stir in the remaining pan juices and enough of the reserved stock to make 2 cups. Cook and stir the gravy until smooth, and simmer for 5 minutes.

Yield: 4 servings.

Each serving provides: 209 cal, 23 g pro, 1.2 g sat fat, 6.2 g unsat fat, 74 mg chol.

Raisin and Rum Chicken in Creamy Almond Sauce

A poem for the palate—a sure winner. Even the picky eaters lick the platter clean. Serve with steamed brown rice, baked potatoes, or mammaligge (cornmeal mush) to soak up every bit of the delicious sauce.

3 tablespoons raisins	¾ cup defatted, low-sodium
3 tablespoons rum	chicken broth
4 whole chicken breasts,	¼ cup almonds, toasted
halved and boned	½ cup apple juice
¼ teaspoon each ginger, dry	½ teaspoon grated orange rind
mustard, and thyme	2 tablespoons chopped
¼ teaspoon pepper	almonds, toasted

In a small bowl, soak the raisins in the rum.

Heat a large, heavy skillet. Remove all visible fat from the chicken breasts and render the fat in the heated skillet. If there is more than 1 tablespoon, remove it and reserve for another use. Add the chicken to the skillet; sprinkle with the herbs and pepper. Cook over medium heat, turning often for about 10 minutes or until the flesh is firm. Remove to a plate and keep warm.

Add the broth to the skillet and bring to a boil. In a blender or food processor, blend the almonds, apple juice, and orange rind.

Add the almond mixture to the skillet, stirring constantly. Simmer for 3 minutes, then stir in the rum and raisins. Taste-check for seasoning.

Reheat the cutlets gently in the hot sauce. Arrange in a heated serving dish, and spoon the sauce over all. Sprinkle with the chopped almonds.

Yield: 8 servings.

Each serving provides: 325 cal, 17.9 g pro, 2.8 g sat fat, 7.6 g unsat fat, 71 mg chol, 70 mg sodium.

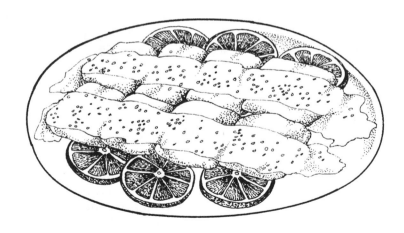

4
TASTY WAYS WITH
CHICKEN PARTS

Chicken with 30 Cloves of Garlic
Aunt Betty's Luscious Chicken with Mushrooms and Rice
Apricot and Almond Stuffed Thighs with Tofu Mustard Sauce
Presto Crunchy Drumsticks
Sesame Almond Sexy Legs
Stuffed Broiled Chicken Legs Rosemary

In our house, the children go for the drumstick; their parents go for a nice, plump thigh. For our family and for entertaining, I find that when I serve a chorus line of beautiful legs, no one is denied his or her favorite part, and everybody feels like dancing.

Chicken with 30 Cloves of Garlic

This is based on a very old recipe that called for 40 cloves of garlic. I ran out of cloves and courage when I got to 30-something. But don't be intimidated. Garlic has so many health benefits, some proven, some reputed. In Russia it is used like we use antibiotics. Eleanor Roosevelt claimed that it helped her memory. It has been shown to tame high blood pressure and lower cholesterol, and a recent survey reveals that garlic eaters have more immunity against the development of cancer. How nice to get all those benefits at one meal!

As for the taste, you'll find that the long cooking has given the garlic a delicious, creamy quality and tamed its pungency. Spread it on hot toast for a treat that warrants a standing ovation.

6 chicken legs with thighs, washed and thoroughly dried
30 cloves garlic, peeled and left whole
3 stalks celery, washed and sliced
½ cup chicken broth
½ teaspoon dried thyme
½ teaspoon freshly grated ginger root or ¼ teaspoon dried
¼ teaspoon freshly ground pepper
½ teaspoon paprika
1 teaspoon herbal seasoning

Preheat the oven to 350°F.

Heat a heavy casserole with a tight-fitting lid. Coat the bottom with nonstick baking spray. Place the chicken in the casserole and brown the chicken about 5 minutes on each side. Add the garlic and the celery, then the chicken broth. Add the thyme, ginger root, pepper, paprika, and herbal seasoning.

Cover the casserole tightly and bake for 1½ hours.

Yield: 6 servings.

Each drumstick provides: 100 cal, 16 g pro, 1.5 g sat fat, 3.9 g unsat fat, 70 mg chol, 248 mg sodium.

Each thigh provides: 142 cal, 16 g pro, 2 g sat fat, 3.9 g unsat fat, 70 mg chol, 248 mg sodium.

Aunt Betty's Luscious Chicken with Mushrooms and Rice

Serve with a crisp green salad and you have a complete meal—deliciously succulent, high in fiber, and rich in cholesterol-reducing nutrients.

1 tablespoon olive, peanut, or canola oil

4 drumsticks and 4 thighs, washed and dried

1 cup chopped onions

1 cup mushrooms, cleaned and sliced

1 clove garlic, minced

¼ teaspoon cayenne pepper

½ teaspoon crushed, dried thyme

½ teaspoon paprika

¼ teaspoon dry mustard (optional)

¼ teaspoon freshly ground pepper

1 cup brown rice, parboiled for 20 minutes

1 can (1 pound) tomatoes

1 large green pepper, sliced

Heat the oil in a heavy skillet. Brown the chicken. Add the onions, mushrooms, garlic, and cayenne pepper. Lightly sauté until the onions are golden—about 3 minutes.

Add the thyme, paprika, mustard, ground pepper, rice, tomatoes, and 2 cups of water or chicken broth. Bring to a boil, then reduce heat and cover. Simmer 20 minutes. Add the sliced pepper and cook, covered, for 10 minutes longer or until the chicken is tender and the peppers are still crisp-tender. Serve piping hot right from the skillet. **Yield:** 8 servings.

Each drumstick provides: 212 cal, 17.8 g pro, 2 g sat fat, 5 g unsat fat, 75 mg chol, 73 mg sodium.

Each thigh provides: 239 cal, 17.8 g pro, 2.5 g sat fat, 5.9 g unsat fat, 75 mg chol, 73 mg sodium.

Apricot and Almond Stuffed Thighs
with Tofu Mustard Sauce

8 chicken thighs
16 dried apricot halves
½ cup slivered almonds,
   toasted
1 teaspoon herbal seasoning
1 tablespoon minced onion
2 cups cooked brown rice

½ cup tofu
4 tablespoons fruit
   juice-sweetened apricot
   preserves
1 tablespoon prepared mustard
   (preferably salt-free)

Preheat oven to 375°F.

Loosen the skin on the thighs. Place 2 apricot halves and 1 tablespoon of slivered almonds under the skin of each thigh. Sprinkle the thighs with the herbal seasoning and onion.

Place the thighs skin side up in a baking pan coated with nonstick cooking spray and bake for 40 to 45 minutes.

To make the sauce, combine the tofu, apricot preserves, and mustard, and heat but do not boil.

Serve the chicken on hot rice and pass the sauce.

Yield: 8 servings.

Each serving without sauce provides: 269 cal, 17.3 g pro, 3.3 g sat fat, 8 g unsat fat, 70 mg chol, 73 mg sodium.

Each tablespoon of sauce provides: 30 cal, 0.7 g pro, no fat, no chol, 13 mg sodium.

Presto Crunchy Drumsticks

So easy to prepare and ready in a hurry. Great for spur-of-the-moment get-togethers and very popular with young people. Great with stewed tomatoes and fresh carrot sticks.

8 drumsticks
½ cup chicken stock
½ cup shredded wheat
*   minibiscuits, crushed*

½ teaspoon cayenne pepper

Preheat oven to 375°F.

Dip the drumsticks in the chicken stock, then roll them in the crushed biscuits mixed with the cayenne pepper. Bake for 30 minutes or until golden brown and crunchy.

Yield: 8 servings.

Each serving provides: 101 cal, 13.7 g pro, 1.5 g sat fat, 3 g unsat fat, 75 mg chol, 88 mg sodium.

Sesame Almond Sexy Legs

Sesame seeds were used by Egyptian sirens to enhance their sex appeal. Oat bran crunch provides cholesterol-lowering fiber. So think lovely thoughts while you indulge in this sensual dish.

¾ cup oat bran crunch,
    crushed
½ cup toasted sesame seeds
½ cup slivered almonds
1 tablespoon dried green
    onions

1 teaspoon dry mustard
½ teaspoon parsley flakes
½ teaspoon dried thyme
8 whole chicken legs
    (drumsticks and thighs)
1 cup pineapple juice

Preheat oven to 350°F.

Combine all the ingredients except the chicken and the pineapple juice. Dip the chicken in the pineapple juice, then coat with the crumb mixture. Place the chicken in a baking dish coated with nonstick cooking spray. Sprinkle with any remaining crumbs. Bake 45 minutes or until the chicken is tender.

Yield: Servings for 8 hearty eaters.

Each leg provides: 219 cal, 30 g pro, 1.4 g sat fat, 6 g unsat fat, 150 mg chol, 75 mg sodium.

Stuffed Broiled Chicken Legs Rosemary

Simply sensational—a great party dish. Serve with cranberry chutney and sweet potato, apple, and granola casserole.

8 whole chicken legs
1½ teaspoons sodium-free herbal
    seasoner
    freshly ground pepper
2 tablespoons chicken fat or
    canola oil

¼ cup lemon or lime juice
2 teaspoons dried rosemary
2 teaspoons prepared mustard
    garnish: parsley and 1
      orange, sectioned

Carefully pull the skin of the thigh away from the meat. Sprinkle the flesh with herbal seasoner and pepper.

Blend together the chicken fat or oil with the lemon or lime juice, rosemary, and mustard. Spread about 2 teaspoons of this mixture under the skin of each thigh.

Place the chicken pieces, skin side down, in a broiling pan coated with nonstick cooking spray. Broil about 6 inches from the heat source for about 14 minutes, or until brown. Turn and broil the other side for another 14 minutes.

To serve, spread any remaining rosemary mixture on the chicken, place on a serving platter, pour the pan juices over the chicken, and garnish the platter with parsley and orange sections.

Yield: 8 servings.

Each serving provides: 200 cal, 24 g pro, 2 g sat fat, 3.04 g unsat fat, 150 mg chol, 85 mg sodium.

5
WINNING WAYS WITH WINGS

Sesame Chicken Wing Appetizers
Crockpot Winning Wings in Chinese Sweet and Sour Sauce
Salt-Free Ketchup
Winged Victory with Pineapple and Sweet Potatoes
Apples on the Wings
Ambrosia Rice Pudding

Learn to go creative with wings and you'll win the battle of the budget. Wings can precede the meal as an appetizer or make the meal as a substantial entrée. There are approximately 9 wings in a pound. A plain wing provides 82 calories, almost 9 grams of protein, 28 mg of cholesterol, and 27 mg of sodium.

Sesame Chicken Wing Appetizers

Delectable succulence that adds pizzazz to your party. Make them ahead, then reheat in the microwave.

12 chicken wings, disjointed and tips removed
1 tablespoon olive, canola, or peanut oil
2 cloves garlic, crushed
2 slices fresh ginger root cut into very fine shreds
2 tablespoons Tamari soy sauce
2 tablespoons dry sherry

2 teaspoons Old Bay seasoning or herbal seasoner (optional)
¼ teaspoon freshly ground pepper
1 tablespoon toasted sesame seeds
2 tablespoons chopped green onions, including the green part

In a wok or skillet, heat the oil and add the garlic and ginger root. Stir briefly, then add the chicken wings. Cook, stirring, until lightly browned, about 3 minutes. Add the soy sauce and sherry and cook, stirring, about 30 seconds longer.

Cover and simmer about 10 minutes. Uncover, turn the heat to

high, and continue cooking, stirring, until the liquid is almost evapo-
rated and the chicken pieces are glazed.

Remove from the heat and add the seasoning or seasoner and
pepper. Toss. Just before serving, toss in the sesame seeds and
onions.

Yield: 12 appetizer servings.
*Each serving provides: 95 cal, 8.7 g pro. 1.2 g sat fat, 3.1 g unsat fat, 28 mg
chol, 197 mg sodium.*

Crockpot Winning Wings
in Chinese Sweet and Sour Sauce

A great no-fuss, do-ahead dish for a summer party, or for taking a
winning covered dish, or to keep the buffet hot and spicy. The
peanut butter adds an interesting Thailand flavor but can be omitted
without changing the sweet and sour concept.

16 chicken wings
4 tablespoons wine or
balsamic vinegar
1 cup fruit juice-sweetened
apricot conserves
2 tablespoons peanut butter
(optional)

1 cup ketchup (see recipe for
salt-free ketchup)
4 tablespoons prepared
horseradish
1 cup finely chopped sweet
onion
1 teaspoon hot sauce (optional)

Pat the chicken wings dry and place them in the Crockpot. In a bowl,
mix together the remaining ingredients. Taste-check for a good bal-
ance of sweet and sour.

Pour the sauce over the wings. Cover the Crockpot and cook on low until the chicken is tender, usually 4 hours.

Yield: 16 flavorful wings.

Each wing provides: 160 cal, 8.8 g pro, 1 g sat fat, 7 g unsat fat, 28 mg chol, 220 mg sodium.

Salt-Free Ketchup

4 cups fresh or canned,
   unsalted tomatoes
¾ cup tomato paste
   (unsalted)
1 cup chopped onions
1 small green pepper, cut into
   small cubes
2 tablespoons honey
1 bay leaf

¼ teaspoon each ground
   cloves, ground allspice,
   ground mace, dry
   mustard, and freshly
   ground black pepper
⅛ teaspoon cinnamon
1 teaspoon minced garlic
¼ cup malt or apple cider
   vinegar

In a saucepan, combine the tomatoes, tomato paste, onions, and green pepper. Bring to a boil and simmer for 30 minutes.

Put this mixture through a food mill, food processor, or blender and process thoroughly.

Return the blended sauce to the saucepan and add the remaining ingredients. Bring to a boil, then simmer, stirring frequently for about 10 minutes.

Yield: About 5 cups.

Each tablespoon provides: 8 cal, no fat, no chol, 2 mg sodium.

Winged Victory
with Pineapple and Sweet Potatoes

½ cup whole wheat flour
¼ cup oat bran
1 teaspoon Old Bay seasoning
  or any good herbal
  seasoner
¼ teaspoon freshly ground
  pepper
16 chicken wings
½ cup chicken broth
1 tablespoon olive or canola
  oil or chicken fat

3 medium-size sweet potatoes
  or yams, steamed and
  peeled
1 (1-pound) can unsweetened
  pineapple chunks;
  reserve syrup
1 teaspoon Tamari soy sauce
3 tablespoons fruit
  juice-sweetened orange
  marmalade

In a clean paper bag, combine the flour, oat bran, seasoning or seasoner, and pepper. Dip the wings in the chicken broth, then shake with the flour mixture in the bag to coat.

Heat the oil or chicken fat in a baking dish in a 425°F oven. Arrange the wings in the pan and brown on each side (about 10 minutes on each side).

Remove the pan from the oven and intersperse the yams or sweet potatoes and pineapple chunks around the wings.

Combine the reserved pineapple juice, soy sauce, and marmalade, and spoon over all. Return to the oven and bake for another 20 minutes.

Yield: 8 servings.

Each serving provides: 234 cal, 18 g pro, 3.2 g sat fat, 4.5 g unsat fat, 56 mg chol, 115 mg sodium.

Apples on the Wings

A real winner in the low-calorie, low-fat department. Apples are a rich source of pectin, which has been shown to escort the harmful factor of cholesterol out of the body. Ambrosia rice pudding makes a delicious accompaniment.

16 chicken wings, washed and dried

2 large apples, scrubbed, unpeeled, sliced

½ teaspoon ground cinnamon

1 teaspoon lemon juice

1 teaspoon honey

1 cup apple juice or apple cider

½ teaspoon Old Bay seasoning or a good herbal seasoner

¼ teaspoon freshly ground pepper

Arrange the wings in a heatproof casserole in a single layer. Combine the apples, cinnamon, lemon juice, and honey. Place the apple mixture over the wings. Combine the apple juice and seasonings and pour over all. Cover the casserole and bake in a 350°F oven for about 50 minutes, or until the wings are tender.

Yield: 16 wings.

Each wing provides: 100 cal, 8.8 g pro, 1.5 g sat fat, 3 g unsat fat, 28 mg chol, 28 mg sodium.

Ambrosia Rice Pudding

1 can (20 ounces) pineapple
    chunks in juice
2 cups cooked brown rice
2 teaspoons grated orange
    rind
2 navel oranges, peeled and
    sectioned

1 banana, thinly sliced
½ cup fresh blueberries or
    sliced strawberries
2 tablespoons flaked coconut
    (unsweetened)

Drain the pineapple juice into a medium-size saucepan. Reserve the chunks. Bring the juice to a boil and stir in the rice. Remove from the heat, cover, and let cool.

Combine the pineapple, orange rind and orange sections, banana, berries, coconut, and rice in a glass bowl. Refrigerate for several hours.

Yield: 10 servings.

Each serving provides: 111 calories, 1 g pro, 1 g fat, no chol, 3 mg sodium.

6
HEARTY, HEALING CHICKEN SOUPS

Basic Poultry Stock
Chicken Stock and a Hearty Soup
Chicken Egg Drop Soup
Mushroom, Barley, and Bean Chicken Soup
Hawaiian Luau Bisque
Chicken Bouillabaisse

Prepare a good, hearty, flavorful soup and you've got it made. Soup warms the bones, cheers the heart, and is the oldest-known remedy for a cold.

There's no better vehicle than soup for enriching your body with important nutrients, for lifting your spirits, and for making recalcitrant eaters healthy when they're not looking.

Chicken soup—Jewish soul food and psychological medicine—can be hot, filling, cheering, satisfying, and custom-made. It can provide trace minerals, vitamins, and fiber and make you feel full and satisfied on very few calories.

You're getting a lot more out of that bowl of soup than a tantalizing aroma and a great blend of flavors. "Soup is the ideal replacement fluid," says Dr. George E. Burch in the February 1976 *American Heart Journal*. "Because vegetables, grains, and meats release their goodness into the fluid in which they are steeped, soup contains everything one finds in plant and animal tissues."

Almost all soups call for chicken broth or stock. Make a big pot of good, hearty chicken broth, cool and store jars of it in the freezer, or cool it and pour into ice cube trays. When the cubes are frozen solid, store them in a plastic bag tightly secured with a twistem or rubber band. Store in the freezer and use frequently to enrich soups or stews, to flavor cooked rice, or to replace fat in a stir-fry. It's liquid gold and better than money in the bank.

Basic Poultry Stock

The addition of an acid such as vinegar helps to release the calcium from the bones, thus enriching the broth. The veal bones enrich the flavor and give this broth more gusto.

1 chicken, duck, or turkey carcass, broken apart (can be cooked or uncooked)

giblets, gizzards, wings, and necks (no liver)

chicken feet (if you can find them) dipped in boiling water and outer skin removed

1 pound veal bones, chopped into 2-inch pieces

3 quarts cold water, or to cover

1 large onion—skin, too—stuck with 2 cloves

1 carrot, quartered

3 stalks celery, including leaves, cut up

2 parsnips, pealed and sliced

1 parsley root, pealed and sliced (optional)

3 to 4 leeks, cleaned and cut into ½-inch pieces

2 bay leaves

½ teaspoon dried thyme

¼ teaspoon freshly grated nutmeg

6 peppercorns

6 sprigs parsley

3 sprigs fresh dill

1 teaspoon herbed or cider vinegar

1 clove garlic, halved

⅛ teaspoon poultry seasoning

In an 8-quart soup pot, combine the carcass, chicken parts, veal bones, and water. Bring to a boil, reduce the heat, and skim off any scum that has come to the surface.

Add the remaining ingredients and simmer for 3 to 4 hours, uncovered.

Strain the stock through a fine sieve. Cool quickly by placing the pot in a sink half filled with very cold water or over ice cubes. When cold, remove all the surface fat. Pour the broth into ice cube trays or pint jars and freeze.

Yield: About 6 cups.

One cup provides: 39 cal, 3.36 g pro, 0.48 g fat, no chol, 600 mg sodium.

Microwave Method

The microwave does a good job of making stock in a hurry. Make it in 2 batches. Use a large casserole-type dish. Cover tightly and microcook on high for about 20 minutes, stirring midway. Let stand for another 20 minutes, then strain.

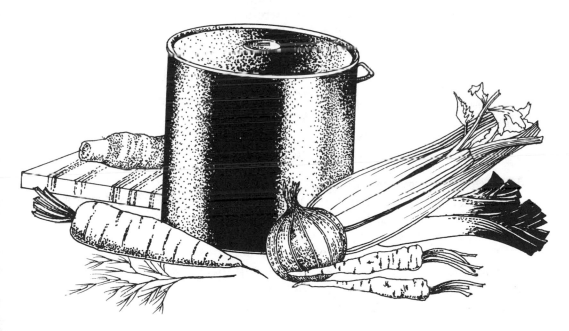

Chicken Stock and a Hearty Soup

1 medium stewing chicken,
    cut into pieces
chicken giblets (not the
    liver)
water to cover
1 large onion, including the
    skin
2 carrots, cut in quarters

¼ cup lemon juice
¼ teaspoon each of freshly
    ground pepper, paprika,
    basil, tarragon, and
    ginger
½ cup chopped parsley
2 stalks celery, including
    leaves, sliced

Wash the chicken and place in a deep pot. Cover with the water. Bring to a boil and skim. Add the remaining ingredients. Cover. Return to a boil, then lower the heat and simmer for 2 hours. Let the chicken cool in the soup; then skin the chicken, bone it, and refrigerate for another dish. Or strain, reserving the chicken and vegetables. Now you have several options: If you're serving the broth as broth, add some cooked brown rice, barley, or noodles and some chopped-up chicken and giblets.

Yield: About 10 servings.
Each serving provides: 39 cal, 3 g pro, 0.48 g fat, no chol, 130 mg sodium.

Variation: Or you can make a very special eggnog that my mom always served to us when we had the sniffles or were convalescing from childhood diseases or the grippe (now called the flu). You feel stronger as you sip it.

    In a soup bowl or in a food processor, beat an egg till frothy. Continue to beat as you slowly add a cup of hot broth. For adults, top with garlicky croutons. (If there is any danger of salmonella in your area, omit the egg.)

Chicken Egg Drop Soup

For extra crunch, fiber, calcium, and beta-carotene, stir in a cup of shredded romaine or escarole lettuce just before serving.

6 cups chicken broth	1 teaspoon soy sauce
2 tablespoons chopped parsley	2 eggs

In a 3-quart saucepan over medium-high heat, heat the broth and the soy sauce to boiling.

Meanwhile, in a small bowl, beat the eggs slightly. Slowly, with a fork, stir the eggs into the boiling soup, and stir until the eggs separate into shreds.

Yield: 6 servings.

Each serving provides: 45 cal, 5.5 g pro, 3.4 g sat fat, 1.8 g unsat fat, 88 mg chol, 640 mg sodium.

Mushroom, Barley, and Bean Chicken Soup

Practically a meal in a dish. The barley gives this soup a hearty, creamy, chewy texture that makes you think it must be fattening. Not so. It actually has less fat and more iron than brown rice. You can enjoy a half cup of cooked barley—with all its calcium, potassium, and niacin—at a cost of only 52 calories. Dried mushrooms add an incomparable flavor to this soup as well as the antistress vitamin pantothenate, niacin, riboflavin, copper, and selenium, which is a valuable antiaging antioxidant.

½ cup large dry lima beans
¼ cup mung beans or brown lentils
¼ cup coarse barley
2 quarts water or stock, including the giblets (but not the liver)
1 3-pound chicken, cut up
3 marrow bones
2 cloves garlic
2 tablespoons dried mushrooms

1 large onion, diced
2 ribs celery with leaves, sliced
1 cup chopped carrots
1 turnip or ½ rutabaga, chopped
½ cup chopped fresh parsley or 2 tablespoons dried
3 sprigs of fresh dill or 1 teaspoon dried
1½ teaspoons Tamari soy sauce

Wash the beans and barley and place in a large soup kettle with the water or stock, chicken, and marrow bones rubbed with the garlic. Bring to a boil and skim. Add the remaining ingredients, cover, and allow to simmer gently (make the pot smile) for about 2 hours or until the beans are soft. Remove the chicken and serve separately.

Yield: 10 servings.

Each serving provides: 51 cal, 2.3 g pro, 1.9 g unsat fat, about 400 mg sodium.

NOTE: If your family doesn't particularly relish boiled chicken, remove the chicken after 45 minutes of cooking in the soup. Put the chicken in a baking dish; rub with garlic; and sprinkle with lemon juice, paprika, ginger, thyme, dry mustard, and a little bit of sage. Roast in a preheated 350°F oven, uncovered, until delicately browned.

Hawaiian Luau Bisque

It may sound strange, but it's simply wonderful!

6 cups chicken stock
3 carrots, scrubbed, cut in
    chunks and slightly
    steamed, or microwaved,
    covered, on high for 3
    minutes

⅓ cup peanut butter
½ cup soft tofu
3 tablespoons light rum
¼ cup unsweetened shredded
    coconut, shredded raw
    carrots, or flaked chicken

In a large soup pot, heat the chicken stock. In a bowl or in the food processor, blend the carrots, peanut butter, and tofu. Blend this mixture into 1 cup of the hot stock, then add this mixture to the remainder of the stock, stirring constantly until smooth and creamy. Add the rum. Serve very hot with a topping of coconut, shredded carrots, or flaked chicken.

Yield: 10 servings.

Each serving provides: 92 cal, 4.5 g pro, 1 g sat fat, 3 g unsat fat, trace of chol, 651 mg sodium.

Chicken Bouillabaisse

Much less expensive than the Mediterranean version but just as delicious!

3 cups chicken broth or water
3 onions, chopped
1 onion, studded with 4
    cloves
1 clove garlic, minced
½ cup chopped celery
4 parsley sprigs, chopped
1 tablespoon fresh thyme or 1
    teaspoon dried
1 broiler-fryer, about 3
    pounds
2 shallots or scallions,
    chopped

1 can (1 pound) tomatoes,
    undrained
½ teaspoon saffron threads
    (optional)
1 teaspoon honey
1⅓ cups dry white wine
6 slices French bread or
    challah, toasted, and
    rubbed with garlic on
    both sides

In a large soup kettle, combine the chicken broth or water, onions, garlic, celery, parsley, and thyme. Bring to a boil and simmer for 30 minutes.

Remove the skin and visible fat from the chicken. Cut into small-ish pieces.

In a skillet, render the fat from the chicken skin. Remove the cracklings and reserve for another use. Sauté the shallots or scallions lightly in the same skillet. Remove from the skillet and reserve. Cut the chicken into small pieces and brown in the same skillet, turning once. Cook uncovered for about 10 minutes.

With a fork, break up the pieces of tomato and add to the chicken.

Cook for 5 minutes. Add the chicken mixture to the soup kettle with the shallots or scallions, saffron, honey, and wine. Discard the clove-studded onion. Cook over low heat for about 1 hour or until the chicken is tender.

To serve, place a slice of toasted French bread or challah, rubbed on both sides with garlic, in each serving bowl. Spoon some chicken and soup over each.

Yield: 6 servings.

Each serving provides: 248 cal, 37 g pro, 2 g sat fat, 4 g unsat fat, 66 mg chol, 467 mg sodium.

7

SAUTÉED, POACHED, AND GRILLED CHICKEN

Crunchy Chicken Cutlets: A Romantic Dinner for Two
Chicken Sauté with Eggplant and Peanuts
Lime and Garlic Chicken
Bulgur-Sprouts Pilaf with Almonds
Grilled Chicken Oregano (low-sodium and very low in calories)
Coolfont Broiled Chicken Breasts with Brown and Wild Rice and Zesty Tomato Sauce
Grilled Chicken with Herbs and Walnuts
Braised Chicken with Burgundy
Poaching

Enjoy the smart alternative to deep-fat fried chicken. The crunchy, gusty, irresistible succulence of the reduced-calorie recipes in this chapter will take you from the Caribbean to Kentucky, New Orleans, and Tanzania, and in good health all the way.

Crunchy Chicken Cutlets: A Romantic Dinner for Two

A smart alternative to costly veal cutlets, with added heart-healthy fiber. Serve with baked sweet potatoes and cranberry chutney.

1 *chicken breast, boned, cut in half and skinned (reserve the skin and bones for stock or rendering)*	2 *tablespoons oat bran*
	2 *tablespoons crushed shredded wheat or wheat germ*
	1 *tablespoon olive, peanut, or canola oil*
1 *egg*	1 *tablespoon chicken fat*
2 *tablespoons water*	*juice of 1 lemon*
pinch of cayenne pepper	2 *tablespoons chopped parsley*

Flatten the cutlets by pounding with a mallet or a heavy skillet until about ½-inch thick.

Beat the egg with the water and the cayenne pepper. On a piece of waxed paper, combine the oat bran and crushed shredded wheat or wheat germ.

Dip the cutlets into the egg mixture, then coat with the oat bran-wheat mixture.

In a large skillet, heat the oil and chicken fat. Add the chicken cutlets and sauté for about 3 minutes on each side, or until the meat is no longer pink all the way through. Test by cutting into them.

Transfer to a serving platter and keep warm. Pour the lemon juice into the skillet and cook over high heat for about 1 minute, stirring constantly. Stir in the parsley. Pour the sauce over the chicken and serve.

Yield: 2 servings.

Each serving provides: 331 cal, 29 g pro, 2.58 g sat fat, 3.86 g unsat fat, 200 mg chol, 203 mg sodium.

Chicken Sauté with Eggplant and Peanuts

Out of Africa with a zingy flavor. Great with brown rice or kasha.

1 tablespoon olive, peanut, or canola oil
1 tablespoon chicken fat
1 chicken, about 3 pounds, cut into 8 pieces
1 large onion, diced
3 cloves garlic, minced
2 medium-size eggplants, cut into 1-inch cubes
1 tablespoon whole wheat flour

1½ cups chicken stock
½ cup dry white wine
½ cup shelled unsalted peanuts
3 bay leaves
⅛ teaspoon cayenne pepper
½ teaspoon dried thyme
¼ teaspoon dried sage
¼ teaspoon dried ginger
¼ teaspoon freshly ground pepper

In a large skillet heat the oil and chicken fat. Add the chicken pieces. Brown on both sides. Add the onion, garlic, and eggplants. Sauté for 3 minutes. Dust with the flour. Add the chicken stock and wine.

Bring to a boil, then reduce the heat to medium. Add the remaining ingredients. Cover the skillet and cook for about 45 minutes or until the chicken is tender.

Remove the chicken to a serving platter. Remove the bay leaves. Pour the sauce with the peanuts over the chicken and serve.

Yield: 6 servings.

Each serving provides: 196 cal, 20 g pro, 1 g sat fat, 2.2 g unsat fat, 85 mg chol, 329 mg sodium.

Lime and Garlic Chicken

This low-calorie delight is always a favorite at our house. If you don't have chicken breasts on hand, substitute legs, drumsticks, or a cut-up broiler-fryer. Serve with a bulgur-sprouts pilaf (the recipe follows).

¼ cup lime juice	1 tablespoon Worcestershire
½ cup reduced-sodium soy	sauce
sauce	2 chicken breasts, halved,
½ teaspoon ground mustard	boned, and skinned
½ teaspoon ground pepper	

Mix together all the ingredients except the chicken. Pour the sauce over the chicken. Cover and marinate in the refrigerator for at least 30 minutes. Spray a skillet with nonstick cooking spray. Add the chicken and cook for 6 minutes on each side. Test for doneness. It should be opaque all the way through.

Yield: 4 servings.

Each serving provides: 130 cal, 25 g pro, 1.5 g fat, 75.5 mg chol, 489 mg sodium.

Bulgur-Sprouts Pilaf with Almonds

A lovely marriage of flavors and textures. Almonds provide a touch of elegance as well as several B vitamins, calcium, iron, and magnesium. Bean sprouts provide a taste of spring, fantastic nutrients, and fiber. When paired with a grain like bulgur, they greatly enhance the quality of the protein.

1 cup bulgur
1 cup fresh mushrooms, sliced
1 tablespoon olive, peanut, or
    canola oil
3 cups vegetable or chicken
    broth
2 medium carrots, shredded

½ teaspoon vegetable seasoner
1½ cups mung bean or alfalfa
    sprouts
½ large green or red pepper,
    chopped
½ cup chopped almonds

In a large casserole, sauté the bulgur and mushrooms in the oil for 5 minutes or until lightly browned. Stir in the broth, carrots, and seasoning. Bring to a boil. Cover and place in a preheated 350°F oven for 20 minutes or until the broth is absorbed, stirring occasionally. Add the sprouts and pepper. Return to the oven for 5 more minutes, then add the almonds.

Yield: 6 servings.

Each serving provides: 163 cal, 7.2 g pro, 1 g sat fat, 11 g unsat fat, no chol, 417 mg sodium.

Grilled Chicken Oregano
(low-sodium and very low in calories)

The Greeks called oregano "joy of the mountains." The lusty flavor of this dish, which is delicious either grilled over charcoal or broiled in the oven, will bring joy to your taste buds.

4 chicken legs
¼ cup chopped onions
¼ cup lemon juice
⅓ cup low-sodium vegetable cocktail
3 cloves garlic, minced
1 teaspoon dried oregano or 1 tablespoon fresh

½ teaspoon freshly ground pepper
1 teaspoon herbal seasoner
½ teaspoon paprika
2 potatoes, scrubbed, unpeeled, sliced thin (optional)
1 cup mushrooms, washed and dried (optional)

To prepare the chicken for either method, cut away all the visible fat and some of the fatty skin. Set aside. Place the legs in a baking dish sprayed with nonstick cooking spray. Cut 4 slits about ¼-inch deep in the meaty part of each leg.

In a small, heavy skillet, heat the reserved chicken fat and skin. Add the onions. Cook on medium high until the onions and skin are crisp. Watch them carefully—don't let the onions blacken. Remove the crisped onions and cracklings. Reserve the chicken fat that remains in the skillet—it will probably be less than a tablespoon, just enough to contribute an incomparable flavor.

Add the lemon juice, vegetable cocktail, garlic, oregano, pepper, herbal seasoner, and paprika to the skillet and heat until bubbly.

TO CHARCOAL-BROIL: With the skin side down, pour some of the lemon mixture over the chicken and grill about 5 inches from very hot coals. Turn and baste with the mixture frequently for about 40 minutes or until the juices run clear when the thighs are pierced and the meat is fork-tender. After 20 minutes into the grilling, surround the chicken with the sliced potatoes and the mushrooms if you're using them. Turn and baste them, too, with the lemon mixture.

TO BROIL IN THE OVEN: With the skin side up, pour some of the lemon mixture over the chicken and broil at 400°F about 6 inches from the heat source for about 20 minutes, basting 3 times. Add the potatoes and mushrooms. Turn and, basting the chicken and the vegetables 3 times, broil for about 20 minutes or until fork-tender.

Yield: 4 servings.
Each serving with potatoes and mushrooms provides: 271 cal, 29.6 g pro, 3.7 g sat fat, 4.2 g unsat fat, 76 mg chol, 92 mg sodium.

Coolfont Broiled Chicken Breasts with Brown and Wild Rice and Zesty Tomato Sauce

We enjoy this dish, a nutritional powerhouse, at our favorite health retreat in West Virginia. Brown rice is the highest of all grains in the B vitamins. It also provides vitamin A, calcium, and iron and includes the cholesterol-lowering, fiber-rich rice bran. Wild rice, a grass, is richer in protein, minerals, and B vitamins than most grains. The acidity of the tomato sauce helps the body to utilize the minerals more efficiently.

1 cup brown rice
½ cup wild rice

3 boneless chicken breasts, halved, skin on to seal in the flavor and keep the meat moist

In a saucepan, heat 2 cups of water and 1 cup of defatted chicken broth. Add the brown rice and the wild rice and cook for about 40 minutes or until the rice is tender.

Preheat the broiler to 400°F. Broil the chicken breasts about 6 inches below the heat source for about 4 minutes on each side, or until they are fork-tender. Remove the skin. Divide the rice mixture among 6 plates. Place a chicken breast on each plate and serve with a zesty tomato sauce.

Zesty Tomato Sauce

1 cup canned plum tomatoes, drained, diced
1 garlic clove, minced
1 tablespoon minced onion or shallot

1 teaspoon dried basil or 1 tablespoon fresh

In a saucepan, combine all ingredients and simmer for 5 minutes. Serve hot.

Yield: 6 servings.
Each serving with rice and sauce provides: 307 cal, 36.7 g pro, 2 g sat fat, 3.7 g unsat fat, 77 mg chol, 262 mg sodium.

Grilled Chicken with Herbs and Walnuts

A favorite of ours for outdoor grilling. The fantastic aroma of the chicken mingling with the herbs is so appetite-teasing the kids can hardly wait to bite into it.

*2 broiler-fryers, about 2
  pounds each
2 teaspoons dried basil or ½
  cup fresh basil leaves
2 cloves garlic, minced
½ cup walnuts, chopped fine*

*½ teaspoon hot pepper sauce
¼ teaspoon freshly ground
  pepper
1 teaspoon olive or canola oil
1 tablespoon lemon juice
1 tablespoon white wine*

Clean the chickens, then split them in halves. Cut off all the excess fat, loosen the skin, and remove any fat imbedded underneath.

In a small, heavy skillet, render the fat. Remove all but 1 tablespoon of rendered fat and reserve for another use.

Add the basil, garlic, walnuts, hot pepper sauce, and pepper to the fat in the skillet. Reserve 2 tablespoons of this mixture. Press the remaining mixture under the skin of the chickens, reaching as many areas as you can.

When the charcoal is white-hot, grill the chicken skin side up for about 15 minutes.

Add the oil, lemon juice, and wine to the reserved herb mixture. Brush some of this mixture on the underside of the chicken.

Turn the chicken and grill 15 minutes longer, brushing the undersides several times while it is cooking.

Yield: 4 servings.

Each serving provides: 378 cal, 50 g pro, 2.07 g sat fat, 4.14 g unsat fat, 148 mg chol, 133 mg sodium.

Braised Chicken with Burgundy

2 broiler-fryers (about 2 to
   2½ pounds each) cut
   in serving-size pieces
¼ cup whole wheat flour
⅔ cup Burgundy
½ cup chicken stock
1 can (8 ounces) sliced
   mushrooms; reserve the
   liquid

1 can (1 pound) small white
   onions, drained
2 tablespoons chopped parsley
½ teaspoon dried thyme
½ teaspoon dried marjoram
½ teaspoon freshly ground
   pepper
½ teaspoon herbal seasoner

Clean the chicken and remove all visible fat. Set aside.

In a heavy skillet, render the fat. Remove all but 2 tablespoons of fat. If you don't have 2 tablespoons of chicken fat, add olive or canola oil to make 2 tablespoons.

Brown the chicken pieces on all sides. Transfer the chicken to a baking dish.

Add the flour to the drippings in the skillet and blend well. Add the Burgundy, chicken stock, and liquid from the mushrooms. Cook, stirring constantly, until the mixture boils and thickens. Add the onions, thyme, marjoram, pepper, and herbal seasoner.

Yield: 4 servings.

Each serving provides: 290 cal, 52 g pro, 2.07 g sat fat, 4.14 g unsat fat, 66 g chol, 133 mg sodium.

Poaching

Back in the seventeenth century, chicken on the table was a symbol of prosperity. It was good King Henry IV of France who said that everyone in his kingdom should have a chicken in his pot every Sunday.

Chicken cooked in a pot is poached. The pot liquor is good old chicken soup.

How does poaching differ from braising? In braising, the bird is browned in fat beforehand, then simmered in relatively little liquid in a covered pot.

In poaching, more liquid is used, and the liquid is plain water or stock. The art of successful poaching is regulating the temperature of the liquid throughout the cooking process. The bird should be immersed in cold water that is brought slowly to a boil. During the cooking period the liquid should be kept just below the boiling point to prevent the bird from drying out and becoming stringy.

When the chicken is done, skim off any surface fat. Put a slice of toast in each soup plate. For a really zingy taste that will knock your diners' socks off, rub the toast all over with garlic.

8

WONDERFULLY GOOD
CHICKEN POT PIE

Pennsylvania Dutch Chicken Pot Pie
Chicken with Wheat and Oat Bran Dumplings
Chicken in Wine over Noodles
English-Style Chicken Pot Pie
Pie Pastry

Chicken pot pie is practically the soul food of the Pennsylvania Dutch. And why not? It can be soul-satisfying, tummy-warming, and spirit-lifting. And so easy and quick to put together.

Every region and every country has its own version of chicken pot pie. The Pennsylvania Dutch version is made with some member of the pasta family. The British version calls for a pie crust enclosing the steaming aromatic chicken and vegetables.

If you have leftover cooked chicken, your pot pie is half made.

Pennsylvania Dutch Chicken Pot Pie

1 chicken (3½ to 4 pounds) cut into 8 serving pieces
water to cover
1 teaspoon herbal seasoning
¼ teaspoon freshly ground pepper

3 large potatoes, scrubbed, unpeeled, sliced about ½-inch thick
1 large onion, sliced
4 sprigs parsley
1 cup uncooked pot pie bows

In a heavy pot with a tight-fitting lid, simmer the chicken with the water, herbal seasoning, and pepper until the chicken is almost tender (about 25 minutes). Add the potatoes, onion, and parsley. Bring to a boil, then continue to simmer, covered, until the vegetables are not quite done, about 15 minutes. Drop the pot pie bows on top of the potatoes and onion. cover the pot again and simmer for about 20 minutes longer.

Serve in a heated tureen or casserole with the bows on top.

Yield: 6 hearty servings.
Each serving provides: 289 cal, 15 g pro, 2.7 g sat fat, 6.7 g unsat fat, 71 mg chol, 50 mg sodium.

Chicken with Wheat and Oat Bran Dumplings

Follow the recipe for Pennsylvania Dutch chicken pot pie. Instead of topping it with pasta for the last 20 minutes of cooking, top it with these luscious dumplings and enjoy a high-fiber alternative.

1 cup whole wheat flour	2 tablespoons chopped fresh
¼ cup oat bran	parsley
2 teaspoons baking powder	⅔ cup chicken broth

In a small bowl, combine the flour, oat bran, baking powder, and parsley. Gradually add the chicken broth, and stir to blend. Drop heaping tablespoons of dough into the simmering pot of soup or stew. Cover the pot and simmer for 15 to 20 minutes or until the dumplings are soft and mushy on the outside and breadlike on the inside.
Yield: About 8 large dumplings.
Each dumpling provides: 54 cal, 2 g pro, just a trace of fat, no chol, about 25 mg sodium.

Chicken in Wine over Noodles

1 small chicken (about 2 to 2½ pounds), cut into serving pieces
¼ cup whole wheat flour
¼ cup finely chopped onions
1 garlic clove, crushed
¼ teaspoon rosemary
¼ teaspoon marjoram
2 cups low-sodium chicken broth
½ teaspoon freshly ground pepper
1 (1-pound can) tomatoes
1 bay leaf
1 carrot, sliced
1 stalk celery, sliced
1 cup mushrooms, sliced
¼ cup white wine
6 ounces egg noodles

Remove all visible fat and some of the skin from the chicken and render it in a heavy skillet. Remove all but 1 tablespoon of the fat and the chicken cracklings. Reserve for another use.

Dredge the chicken pieces with 2 tablespoons of the flour; sauté until golden. Remove the chicken from the pan. Add the onions to the pan and sauté until soft. Add the garlic, rosemary, and marjoram, and cook for a few minutes longer but do not allow it to brown. Blend in 2 tablespoons of flour. Gradually add the chicken broth and cook, stirring constantly, until thickened. Add the tomatoes, pepper, chicken, bay leaf, carrot, and celery. Simmer slowly for 15 minutes. Add the mushrooms and wine. Bring to a boil. Cover, reduce the heat, and simmer slowly for 30 minutes or until the chicken is tender. Remove the bay leaf.

Cook the noodles and drain. Place on a heated serving dish and top with the chicken. Pour the sauce over all.

Yield: 6 servings.
Each serving provides: 299 cal, 16 g pro, 2.7 g sat fat, 6.7 g unsat fat, 71 mg chol, 572 mg sodium.

English-Style Chicken Pot Pie

In this recipe, the unusually flavorful, heart-healthy pie crust shares honors with the filling.

1 chicken, (about 3½ pounds), cut into 8 serving pieces
1 teaspoon herbal seasoning
½ teaspoon freshly ground pepper
1 cup carrots, scraped and cut into thin rounds
1 cup chopped onions
½ cup chopped celery
1 clove garlic, minced
3 sprigs fresh parsley
¼ teaspoon dried thyme
1 bay leaf

3 tablespoons whole wheat flour
¾ cup dry, white wine
2 cups chicken or vegetable broth or water
⅛ teaspoon freshly ground nutmeg
1 tablespoon Worcestershire sauce
pie pastry (recipe follows)
1 egg yolk
1 tablespoon water

Place the chicken in a heavy casserole, skin side down. Sprinkle with the herbal seasoning and pepper. Cook, uncovered, till just golden brown on one side. Turn the pieces. Scatter the carrots, onions, celery, and garlic over the chicken pieces.

Add the parsley, thyme, bay leaf, and another generous grinding of pepper.

Sprinkle with flour. Stir until the pieces are coated. Add the wine and the broth or water. Bring to a boil. Stir and cover. Reduce the heat to simmer. Simmer for 30 minutes or until the chicken is tender.

Transfer the chicken to a shallow baking dish, preferably an oval dish about 14 × 8 × 2 inches. Scatter the onions on top.

Skim off fat from the sauce in which the chicken cooked. Pour the sauce into a saucepan; add the nutmeg and Worcestershire sauce. Bring the sauce to a boil and pour it over the chicken mixture. Let cool.

Roll out the pastry large enough to more than fit the rim of the baking dish. Fit the pastry over the dish, pressing it tightly onto the rim and outer sides.

Place the dish in an oven preheated to 400°F and bake for 30 minutes.

Pie Pastry

3 heaping tablespoons tahini
or sesame butter
1 cup whole wheat flour

1 teaspoon herbal seasoning
4 tablespoons ice water

In a food processor, combine the tahini or sesame butter, flour, and herbal seasoning.

Start processing and gradually add through the funnel only enough water to make a dough that holds together. Add as little water as possible.

Turn the dough out onto waxed paper and knead briefly. Roll out to fit the baking dish.

Yield: 6 servings.
Each serving provides: 339 cal, 18 g pro, 3.7 g sat fat, 8.7 g unsat fat, 71 mg chol, 572 mg sodium.

Variation: Instead of the tahini or sesame butter crust, you can use a mashed potato crust. Cook 2 medium-size potatoes, mash, and add an egg and 2 tablespoons of chicken broth or water. Spoon evenly over the chicken mixture. Bake in a 350°F oven for 15 minutes.

9
CHICKEN WITH FRUIT

Chicken or Turkey Cutlets with a Delightful Kiwifruit Sauce
Chicken with Prunes
Peachy Chicken Piquant over Fluffy Brown Rice
Honolulu Chicken with Pineapple
Roast Chicken or Turkey Breast with Spicy Cherry Sauce
Chicken with Pineapple, Love, and Wheat Germ
Chicken with Grapes
Chicken with Apricots
Cold Chicken with Avocado Sauce
Savory Grapefruit Chicken
Granny Smith Chicken
Exotic Flavored Pineapple Chicken

It's a wonderful marriage. The fruit brings moisture, flavor, fiber, and important vitamins and minerals to the marriage. The vitamin C in the fruit helps the body to utilize the iron in the chicken. The vitamin C also tenderizes the meat, reducing the cooking time.

Chicken or Turkey Cutlets
with a Delightful Kiwifruit Sauce

Easy to prepare, low-calorie, and nutrient-dense. Wonderful for instant meals. Prepare them when you have a few spare moments, store in the freezer, and you're ready for the hungry hordes.

1 egg white
1 tablespoon water
½ cup dry whole grain bread crumbs, oat bran, or a combination of these
1 teaspoon paprika

½ teaspoon freshly ground pepper
1 pound chicken or turkey breast cutlets, cut in slices ⅛- to ¼-inch thick

SAUCE

⅓ cup fruit juice-sweetened apricot preserves or orange marmalade

2 kiwifruit, pared and sliced
1½ teaspoons prepared horseradish

In a shallow bowl, beat the egg white with the water. Set aside. Combine bread crumbs, oat bran, or combination; the paprika; and the pepper on waxed paper. Dip the cutlets into the egg mixture, then into the crumb mixture. Arrange the breaded cutlets on a baking sheet lined with waxed paper. Place in the freezer for about 30 minutes, then transfer to a freezer bag. Return to the freezer until ready to bake.

When ready to serve, preheat the oven to 400°F. Spray a baking sheet with nonstick cooking spray. Arrange the cutlets on the baking sheet and bake for about 9 minutes for the ⅛-inch slices and for about 10 minutes for the ¼-inch slices or until the meat is no longer pink in the center.

TO MAKE THE SAUCE: Over medium-high heat, heat the apricot preserves in a small saucepan. Stir in the kiwifruit and horseradish. Heat until warm. Serve over cutlets.

TO MAKE THE SAUCE IN THE MICROWAVE: In a small bowl, microcook the marmalade or preserves, covered with waxed paper, for 60 seconds on high. Add the cut-up kiwifruit and the horseradish. Microcook for another 10 seconds or until the sauce is heated.

Yield: 4 servings.
Each serving with 2 tablespoons of sauce provides: 170 cal, 29 g pro, 1 g sat fat, 2.3 unsat fat, 66 mg chol, 60 mg sodium.

Chicken with Prunes

Prunes, the wrinkled plums that have won a reputation as a "morning regular," contribute fiber, lots of immunity-building vitamin A, and a regular gold mine of magnesium, iron, and potassium.

1 3½- to 4-pound chicken,
    whole or cut up
2 teaspoons cumin
1 teaspoon Hungarian paprika
1 clove garlic, minced

½ teaspoon freshly ground
    pepper
1 cup seedless prunes
2 cups water
1 onion, sliced

Wipe the chicken dry with paper towels and place in a heavy casserole or roasting pan. Sprinkle with the cumin, paprika, garlic, and pepper. Allow to sit for 20 minutes so the spices can penetrate. Meanwhile, soak the prunes in the water.

Preheat the oven to 350°F.

Arrange onion slices over and around the chicken. Add the prunes with the soak water. Cover and cook for 1 hour or until the meat is tender and the juices run clear.

Yield: 4 servings.

Each serving provides: 235 cal, 28 g pro, 1 g sat fat, 2.3 g unsat fat, 70 mg chol, 57 mg sodium.

Peachy Chicken Piquant
over Fluffy Brown Rice

Brown rice contains the cholesterol-lowering rice bran as well as the important B vitamins that help you keep your cool and is a good source of magnesium, the nutrient that puts a twinkle in your eye.

12 pieces of chicken (drumsticks, thighs, and/or breast halves)
½ teaspoon freshly ground pepper
¾ cup low-sodium ketchup
1 can (16 ounces) sliced peaches, drained; reserve the juice
1 cup water

2 tablespoons reduced-sodium Tamari soy sauce
1 large onion, sliced
1 large red or green pepper, cut in squares
3 teaspoons arrowroot or cornstarch
¼ cup water
3 cups hot cooked brown rice

Dry the chicken with paper towels and sprinkle with pepper. Place skin side up in a 2½-quart casserole sprayed with nonstick cooking spray.

Bake at 450°F for 20 minutes.

Combine the ketchup, peach syrup, and enough water to make 2 cups. Pour over the chicken. Top with the onion separated into rings.

Cover and bake 30 minutes longer. Add the pepper, peaches, and arrowroot or cornstarch dissolved in ¼ cup water. Cover and bake for 20 more minutes.

Serve with the sauce over hot brown rice.

Yield: 6 servings.
Each serving (2 pieces of chicken and ½ cup rice) provides: 382 cal, 33 g pro, 2 g sat fat, 4 g unsat fat, 70 mg chol, 130 mg sodium.

Honolulu Chicken with Pineapple

Savor the spirit and flavor of Hawaii with this very popular quick-and-easy dish.

1 can (20 ounces) unsweetened pineapple chunks with juice
2 tablespoons reduced-sodium Tamari soy sauce
2 tablespoons lemon juice
1 tablespoon honey
½ teaspoon fresh ginger, minced
1 tablespoon minced onion
1 broiler chicken, cut into 8 parts

In a bowl, combine all the ingredients except the chicken.

Put the chicken in another deep bowl and pour the marinade over it. Refrigerate for 1 hour.

Place the chicken parts in a large baking pan. Pour marinade over the chicken and place in a preheated 350°F oven. Cover and bake for about 1 hour. Remove the cover for the last 15 minutes of baking.

Yield: 6 servings.
Each serving provides: 239 cal, 28 g pro, 1 g sat fat, 2.3 g unsat fat, 66 mg chol, 107 mg sodium.

Roast Chicken or Turkey Breast
with Spicy Cherry Sauce

The breast or breasts are roasted with the skin on to keep the meat moist and flavorful, but the skin is removed before serving.

1 turkey breast or 3 chicken breasts (about 4 pounds)
1 can (16 ounces) pitted Bing cherries, drained; reserve the juice
1 tablespoon vinegar (preferably balsamic)
1 tablespoon honey
½ teaspoon cinnamon
⅛ teaspoon ground cloves
⅛ teaspoon ground nutmeg
¼ teaspoon ground ginger
2 tablespoons arrowroot or cornstarch
¼ cup cold water

Place the washed and dried breasts in a shallow roasting pan. Roast in a preheated 325°F oven for 1½ to 2 hours or until the meat is tender.

Meanwhile, combine in a small saucepan the cherry juice, vinegar, honey, and spices. Bring to a boil, then reduce the heat and cook for 10 minutes.

Mix the arrowroot or cornstarch with ¼ cup of cold water and add it to the hot liquid, stirring constantly until the sauce is thickened. Add the cherries and heat.

Remove the roasted breasts from the oven. Let them rest for about 10 minutes. Remove the skin and slice the meat. Spoon 2 tablespoons of hot cherry sauce over each serving.
Yield: 8 servings.

Each serving provides: 206 cal, 29 g pro, 1 g sat fat, 2.3 g unsat fat, 150 mg chol, 97 mg sodium.

Chicken with Pineapple, Love, and Wheat Germ

Enjoy the slightly oriental flavor of this immensely popular dish. The wheat germ provides morale-boosting B vitamins and valuable fiber. Sesame seeds are high in vitamin E and were used by ancient Egyptian beauties to enhance their sex appeal.

2 large chicken breasts	1 clove garlic
2 tablespoons sesame seeds	1 cup canned pineapple chunks, drained
3 tablespoons wheat germ	
1 tablespoon chicken fat or peanut oil	1 cup hot reduced-sodium chicken broth
1 cup sliced mushrooms	2 tablespoons arrowroot or cornstarch
¼ teaspoon freshly ground pepper	2 cups hot cooked brown rice

Remove skin from the chicken breasts and reserve. Slice the chicken into bite-size chunks.

Render the chicken skin in a large, heavy skillet or wok. Remove all but I tablespoon of fat, or use the peanut oil instead.

Sauté the chicken chunks, sesame seeds, and wheat germ in the fat until the chicken turns white. Add the mushrooms, ground pepper, and garlic. Cook a few minutes longer over medium heat. Add the pineapple chunks.

In a small bowl, dissolve the arrowroot or cornstarch in a few tablespoons of the chicken broth. Stir into the chicken mixture. Cook, stirring, until the sauce thickens. Spoon the mixture over the hot cooked rice.

Yield: 6 servings.

Each serving provides: 239 cal, 22 g pro, 1.4 g sat fat, 4.4 g unsat fat, 45 mg chol, 312 mg sodium.

Chicken with Grapes

So easy, so quick, so good! And so few calories!

1 tablespoon chicken fat or
  peanut oil
4 chicken breasts, split,
  boned, and skinned;
  reserve the skin
1 clove garlic, minced
1 cup chicken or vegetable
  broth
1 tablespoon arrowroot or
  cornstarch

½ teaspoon freshly ground
  pepper
½ teaspoon dried thyme
¼ teaspoon ground ginger
1 cup seedless grapes
2 tablespoons finely chopped
  parsley

In a large skillet, render the chicken skin. Remove all but 1 table-spoon of the fat, or use 1 tablespoon of peanut oil.

Brown the chicken breasts on both sides and remove from the skillet. Remove the pan from the heat. Add the garlic. Dissolve the arrowroot or cornstarch in a few tablespoons of broth and add to the skillet. Stir to blend. Add the remaining stock and stir over moderate heat until the mixture boils. Reduce the heat to simmer; add the pepper, ginger, and thyme; and return the chicken to the skillet. Cover and simmer for about 30 minutes or until the chicken is tender. Add the grapes and parsley and continue cooking until the grapes are warm.

Yield: 8 servings.

Each serving provides: 179 cal, 26 g pro, 1.4 g sat fat, 3.7 g unsat fat, 45 mg chol, 280 mg sodium.

Chicken with Apricots

A delightful one-pot dinner. Apricots bring a festive touch and lots of blood-building iron. The rice cooked in the broth contributes a delectable flavor and lots of cholesterol-lowering rice bran.

1 3-pound broiler-fryer, cut in 8 pieces	½ teaspoon saffron threads (optional)
1 teaspoon dried oregano	1 cup raw brown rice
1½ cups sliced onions	2 cups reduced-sodium chicken broth
1 teaspoon herbal seasoning	
¼ teaspoon freshly ground pepper	⅔ cup dried apricots
⅛ teaspoon cayenne	1 tablespoon lemon juice

Wash and wipe dry the chicken pieces.

Heat, and spray a 6-quart Dutch oven with nonstick cooking spray. Brown the chicken a few pieces at a time, until golden-brown all over. Remove the chicken as it browns.

Preheat the oven to 350°F.

Add the oregano and onions to the Dutch oven. Sauté, stirring over medium heat, until golden—about 3 minutes.

Add seasonings and saffron if you are using it, and rice to the Dutch oven. Cook, stirring, until the rice is golden—about 6 minutes.

Add the chicken broth, apricots, and lemon juice to the rice mixture. Add the chicken pieces. Bring to a boil.

Transfer the pot to the oven and bake, covered, about 1 hour, or until the chicken is tender. Serve hot, directly from the Dutch oven, or arrange the rice on a platter, placing the apricots around the rice and the chicken on top.

Yield: 6 servings.

Each serving of chicken with rice and apricots provides: 241 cal, 11.8 g pro, 2.6 g sat fat, 9.5 g unsat fat, 71 mg chol, 200 mg sodium.

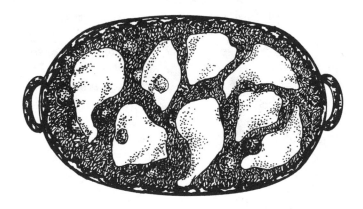

Cold Chicken with Avocado Sauce

Velvety sensual avocado teams up with chicken to form a lovely blend of flavors and texture.

2 whole chicken breasts,
    halved, boned, and
    skinned
    water to cover

4 cloves garlic
½ teaspoon thyme, tarragon,
    or oregano

SAUCE
    ½ cup mashed avocado
    1 tablespoon lemon juice
    1 tablespoon tahini

TO MAKE THE CHICKEN: Flatten each chicken breast with a mallet or a heavy skillet until about ¼-inch thick. Place in a skillet and pour in just enough water to cover. Add the whole garlic cloves and the herb of your choice. Bring to a boil, then reduce to simmer, covered, for about 10 minutes or until the chicken is tender. Remove the chicken from the broth and chill.

TO MAKE THE SAUCE: Combine the avocado, lemon juice, and tahini in a small bowl and beat until smooth. Spread some of the sauce over each breast and roll up. Use a toothpick in each roll to hold its shape. Garnish the top of each with a spoonful of sauce. Serve immediately. **Yield:** 4 servings.
Each serving provides: 212 cal, 27 g pro, 2.5 sat fat, 9 g unsat fat, no chol, no sodium.

Savory Grapefruit Chicken

Grapefruit contributes a palate-pleasing tartness and lots of vitamin C to help you get more mileage out of the minerals in the chicken. It also provides the very important bioflavonoids that help to keep your capillary walls strong.

1 chicken—about 3 pounds— cut in pieces
½ cup plus 2 tablespoons grapefruit juice, divided
2 tablespoons sliced scallions
1 tablespoon chopped parsley
¾ teaspoon herbal seasoning
¼ teaspoon dried marjoram

⅛ teaspoon freshly ground pepper
⅛ teaspoon poultry seasoning
1 large green pepper, cut in chunks
1½ teaspoons arrowroot or cornstarch
1 cup grapefruit sections

Brown the chicken pieces under the broiler, then place them in a large skillet. Add ½ cup of the grapefruit juice, and the scallions, parsley, herbal seasoning, marjoram, pepper, and poultry seasoning. Cover and simmer for 15 minutes. Add the green pepper. Cover and simmer for 15 minutes longer or until the chicken is tender.

With a slotted spoon, remove the chicken and green pepper to a serving platter. Dissolve the arrowroot or cornstarch in the remaining 2 tablespoons of grapefruit juice; add this to the skillet and stir until the sauce boils and thickens. Add the grapefruit sections. Pour the sauce over the chicken.

Yield: 4 servings.

Each serving provides: 152 cal, 25 g pro, 1.28 g sat fat, 2.07 g unsat fat, 70 mg chol, 70 mg sodium.

Granny Smith Chicken

A very-low-calorie, delightful combination of orchard and barnyard.

1 3½- to 4-pound chicken,
    cut in 8 pieces
1 teaspoon herbal seasoner
¼ teaspoon freshly ground
    pepper
1 cup mushrooms, quartered
2 leeks, washed and chopped
1½ cups chicken broth

¼ cup apple juice or cider
1 large Granny Smith apple,
    unpeeled, cored, and
    cut into ¼-inch wedges
1 tablespoon lemon juice
2 tablespoons arrowroot or
    cornstarch

Wash and dry the chicken pieces. Remove all visible fat.

In a large skillet over medium-high heat, render the fat. Sprinkle the chicken with the seasoner and pepper.

Remove all but 1 tablespoon of fat from the skillet. Brown chicken pieces, half at a time, on both sides—about 10 minutes. Remove the chicken pieces to the platter as they brown.

Remove all but 2 tablespoons of drippings from the skillet. Sauté the mushrooms and leeks for 3 minutes. Add 1 cup of chicken broth and the apple juice or cider, stirring to loosen the delicious brown bits from the bottom of the skillet.

Return the chicken to the skillet and bring the liquid just to a boil, then reduce the heat and simmer, covered, for 20 minutes. Add the apple and lemon juice. Cook covered 3 minutes longer or until the apple is tender.

In a small bowl, blend the remaining chicken broth with the

arrowroot or cornstarch. Cook another minute or until the sauce thickens.

Yield: 4 servings.

Each serving provides: 213 cal, 26 g pro, 1.28 g sat fat, 2.6 g unsat fat, 74 mg chol, 317 mg sodium.

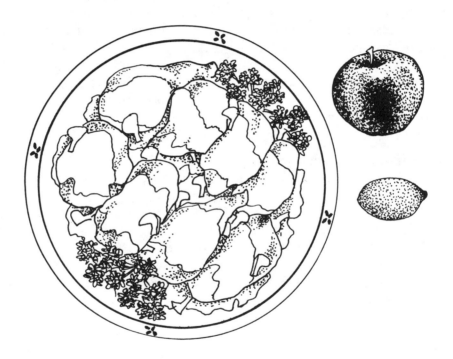

Exotic Flavored Pineapple Chicken

We call this the "chicken that went to college." It's so easy to put together for an impromptu meal for hungry teenagers, and it gets its marvelous, exotic flavor from incongruous ingredients that can be found in practically every pantry.

6 chicken legs (thighs and
    drumsticks) or 2 fryers,
    disjointed
1 cup ketchup (preferably
    homemade, see Index)
1 can (20 ounces) crushed
    pineapple, drained

2 cloves garlic, minced
½ teaspoon ground ginger
¼ teaspoon dry mustard
1 teaspoon herbal seasoning
1 cup freshly brewed
    decaffeinated coffee

Place the chicken in a baking dish or roasting pan. Set aside. Combine all the remaining ingredients in a bowl. Pour this mixture over the chicken.

At this point you can cover the pan and allow it to marinate overnight in the refrigerator, or you can place the pan in a 350°F oven and bake for about an hour or until tender, basting frequently with the delicious sauce.

Yield: 6 servings.

Each serving provides: 230 cal, 28 g pro, 2 g sat fat, 4 g unsat fat, 75 mg chol, 75 mg sodium.

10
EXOTIC ETHNIC DISHES

Hungarian Chicken Paprikash
Latin Chicken with Spaghetti
Chicken Cacciatore
Sombrero Baked Chicken Flavored with Cinnamon and Carob
Iranian Chicken with Pistachios and Sweet Rice
Indonesian Peanut-Studded Chicken
Poached Chicken Parisienne
Cucumber Dressing
South of the Border Curried Chicken with Rice and Jamaican Rum
Yorkshire Batter-Baked Chicken
Left Bank Dijon Chicken
Chicken Tel Aviv
Chicken Sabra with Bing Cherries and Brown Rice
Canton Chicken with Almonds
Israeli Chicken Bake with Matzoh and Dill
Coke 'n' Chicken
Toasty Persian Chicken Balls
Moroccan Chicken Stew with Olives and Avocado
Farfel Chicken Casserole

You can take a gastronomic tour of the world without a backpack and without a travel guide. The recipes in this chapter bring you the fiery taste of Mexico, the peanut-flavored delights of Indonesia, the Old World nostalgic spice of Hungary, the luscious black olives and spicy spaghetti of Italy. All the palate-pleasing delights of a culinary adventure without leaving home, but with a healthy difference: Fat content has been slashed, sugar has been eliminated, and cooking procedures have been simplified. Enjoy!

Hungarian Chicken Paprikash

The sauce permeates the chicken and the noodles for a full-bodied dish of Old World flavor. It can also be served on brown rice or millet for a change of texture and more fiber.

2 broiler-fryers, cut up	1 teaspoon herbal seasoning
1 cup chopped onions	1/4 teaspoon pepper
2 tablespoons paprika	1 can (8 ounces) tomatoes
1 tablespoon whole wheat flour	1 pound broad noodles, cooked

Remove all visible fat and some of the skin from the chickens.

In a large skillet, render the chicken fat and skin. Brown the chicken pieces in the rendered fat. Remove the browned chicken from the skillet and sauté the onions in the pan drippings until soft. Stir in the paprika and the flour. Cook, stirring constantly, for 1 minute. Stir in the herbal seasoning, pepper, and tomatoes. Break up the tomatoes with a wooden spoon.

Add the chicken and giblets (except the liver). Turn to coat each piece. Cover the skillet and simmer for 20 minutes. Turn the chicken pieces and add the liver. Simmer 15 minutes longer or until the chicken is tender.

Place the hot noodles on a serving platter. Arrange the chicken on the noodles. Bring the sauce in the skillet to a boil. Spoon the hot sauce over the noodles and chicken before serving.

Yield: 8 servings.

Each serving provides: 179 cal, 48 g pro, 1 g sat fat, 2 g unsat fat, 75 mg chol, 150 mg sodium.

Latin Chicken with Spaghetti

A colorful and flavorful bless-your-heart dish enriched with oat bran and lecithin and embellished with red pimentos and black olives.

2 broiler-fryers (about 2½ to 3 pounds each), cut in serving-size pieces
½ cup whole wheat flour
½ cup oat bran
2 tablespoons lecithin granules
1 teaspoon herbal seasoning
¼ teaspoon freshly ground pepper
2 cloves garlic, minced
⅓ cup chopped parsley

½ teaspoon poultry seasoning
dash Tabasco sauce
1 cup dry white wine
¼ cup pitted black olives, sliced
½ cup sliced mushrooms
1 jar (4 ounces) red pimentos, drained and cut into 1-inch pieces
1 pound thin spaghetti, cooked

Remove all visible fat and some of the skin from the chickens. Render the fat and skin in a large, heavy skillet. Remove the chicken cracklings and reserve for another use.

On waxed paper, blend together the flour, oat bran, lecithin granules, herbal seasoning, and pepper. Roll the chicken in the seasoned flour mixture, then brown it in the rendered fat.

Blend together the garlic, parsley, poultry seasoning, Tabasco sauce, and wine. Pour over the browned chicken and simmer for 5 minutes.

Scatter the olives, mushrooms, and pimento over the chicken. Cover the skillet and cook over moderately low heat for 30 minutes or until the chicken is tender.

Place the hot spaghetti on a serving dish. Top with the chicken pieces. Pour the hot wine sauce over all.

Yield: 8 servings.

Each serving provides: 270 cal, 48 g pro, 4 g sat fat, 8 g unsat fat, 75 mg chol, 245 mg sodium.

Chicken Cacciatore

1 broiler-fryer, cut up
½ cup chopped onions
½ teaspoon herbal seasoning
¼ teaspoon freshly ground
    pepper
1 clove garlic, minced

1 can (1-pound) tomatoes
1 tablespoon vinegar
    (preferably balsamic)
½ teaspoon rosemary, crumbled
½ teaspoon honey

Remove all visible fat and the fatty pieces of the skin from the chicken and render them in a heavy skillet.

Remove the browned cracklings and all but 1 tablespoon of fat from the skillet. Brown the onions in the fat and remove.

Sprinkle the chicken with the herbal seasoning and the pepper. Add another tablespoon of chicken fat or oil and brown the chicken pieces in the skillet with the garlic.

Add all the remaining ingredients and the browned onions to the skillet. Cover and simmer for 30 minutes or until the chicken is tender.

Yield: 4 servings.

Each serving provides: 170 cal, 22 g pro, 1.5 g sat fat, 2.5 g unsat fat, 65 mg chol, 140 mg sodium.

Sombrero Baked Chicken
Flavored with Cinnamon and Carob

For those who like it hot, this dish will hit the spot. Serve with a cool cucumber salad and a Mexican brown rice and cream-style corn casserole.

1 broiler-fryer (about 2½ to 3 pounds), cut in serving-size pieces	2 tablespoons apricot conserves or orange marmalade
1 teaspoon herbal seasoning	1 tablespoon carob powder or unsweetened cocoa
¼ teaspoon freshly ground pepper	½ teaspoon Tabasco sauce
1 red or green pepper, cut in strips	½ teaspoon cinnamon
1 can (8 ounces) tomato sauce	2 teaspoons sesame seed

Remove all visible fat and some of the fatty skin from the chicken pieces; reserve for future use. Place the chicken pieces in a baking dish in a single layer and sprinkle with the herbal seasoning and pepper.

Place the pepper strips over the chicken.

In a bowl, combine the tomato sauce, apricot conserves or orange marmalade, carob or cocoa, Tabasco sauce, and cinnamon. Sprinkle with the sesame seeds. Cover with foil or parchment paper and bake at 375°F for 45 minutes. Remove the foil or parchment paper and bake 15 minutes longer.

Yield: 8 servings.

Each serving provides: 178 cal, 22 g pro, 1.5 g sat fat, 2.9 g unsat fat, 70 mg chol, 305 mg sodium.

Iranian Chicken with Pistachios and Sweet Rice

2 broiler-fryers (about 2½ to 3 pounds each), cut in serving-size pieces

3 carrots, scraped clean and thinly sliced

4 cups chicken broth, divided

½ cup chopped almonds, lightly toasted (2 minutes in the microwave or 7 minutes in a 350°F oven)

1 tablespoon grated orange rind

2 tablespoons apricot conserves or orange marmalade

2 medium onions, thinly sliced

½ cup chicken broth or water

2 cups long-grain brown rice

⅛ teaspoon freshly ground pepper

½ teaspoon paprika

1 teaspoon herbal seasoning

4 tablespoons unsalted pistachio nuts, chopped

Remove all visible fat and some of the fatty skin from each chicken. In a heavy saucepan, render the fat of one chicken. Remove the crispy cracklings when golden, and reserve.

Add the sliced carrots. Cook over low heat until crisp-tender. Add 1 cup of chicken stock and the almonds, orange rind, and conserves or marmalade. Set aside.

In a heavy 2-quart saucepan with a tight-fitting lid, cook the sliced onions in ½ cup of chicken broth or water until the onions are soft but not browned. Add 3 cups of stock and bring to a boil. Add the rice, herbal seasoning, and carrot mixture. Mix to blend the ingredients, cover tightly, and cook over low heat until the liquid is absorbed and rice is tender, about 40 minutes.

While the rice is cooking, render the fat of the other chicken in a large skillet with a lid. Brown both chickens all over. Sprinkle with the pepper, paprika, and herbal seasoning, and cook over low heat for 10 minutes. Turn the chicken pieces, cover again, and cook 10 minutes longer or until the chicken is tender and the juices run clear.

Spoon 1 cup of the rice mixture on each plate. Top with a serving of chicken, and garnish with chicken cracklings or toasted pistachio nuts.

Yield: 8 servings.

Each serving of chicken and rice provides: 400 cal, 29 g pro, 2 g sat fat, 8 g unsat fat, 70 mg chol, 196 mg sodium.

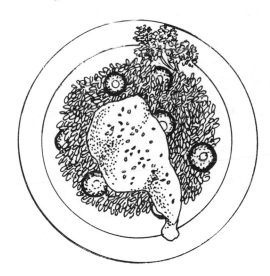

Indonesian Peanut-Studded Chicken

The crunchy oat bran and chopped peanut overcoat on each piece of this moist, flavorful chicken make this a special-occasion dish. Your bypass friends will love it. Serve with a tossed salad and a sweet potato and apple casserole.

1 broiler-fryer, cut up	¾ cup apricot conserves or
1 teaspoon herbal seasoner	orange marmalade
¼ teaspoon freshly ground	1 teaspoon dry mustard
pepper	2 cloves garlic, minced
¾ cup oat bran	½ cup peanuts, finely chopped
1 egg white	

Dust the chicken with the herbal seasoner and the pepper. Place the oat bran on a sheet of waxed paper.

In a soup bowl or on a pie plate, combine the egg white, conserves or marmalade, mustard, and garlic.

Put the chopped peanuts on another piece of waxed paper.

Dip the chicken pieces first in the oat bran, then in the egg mixture, then roll in the chopped peanuts. Place the chicken in a single layer in a baking dish. Bake at 375°F for 40 minutes or until the chicken is tender and the peanuts are golden.

Yield: 4 servings.

Each serving provides: 438 cal, 32 g pro, 2 g sat fat, 12 g unsat fat, 70 mg chol, 117 mg sodium.

Poached Chicken Parisienne

Cool and fruity—a wonderful dish for a patio lunch when the thermometer soars. Apricots are rich in cancer-inhibiting vitamin A and in magnesium, a mineral necessary for the proper functioning of the nerves and muscles, including the heart. Grapes are an excellent source of potassium, especially needed during the hot months when it is depleted through perspiration.

3 whole chicken breasts (about 12 ounces each)
5 or 6 celery leaves
2 teaspoons no-salt herbal seasoner
6 peppercorns
2 bay leaves
1 cup chicken broth
1 cup chopped celery
1 cup seedless green grapes, halved
cucumber dressing (recipe follows)
romaine or Bibb lettuce
6 apricots, washed, halved, and pitted

In a large skillet or saucepan, combine the chicken breasts, celery leaves, herbal seasoner, peppercorns, bay leaves, and chicken broth. Bring to a boil. Cover and simmer for 30 minutes or until the meat is tender.

Allow the chicken to cook in the broth until it is easy to handle, then remove and pull off the skin. Remove the meat from the bones and cut it in cubes. Reserve the broth for another use.

In a large bowl, combine the cut-up chicken, celery, and grapes. Drizzle with about half of the cucumber dressing (see the following recipe). Toss lightly to mix, and chill at least an hour to blend the flavors.

To serve, line a large bowl with lettuce, pile the chicken mixture in the center, frame with the apricot halves, and serve with the remaining dressing.

Yield: 6 servings.

Each serving with 2 tablespoons of dressing provides: 143 cal, 18.6 g pro, 0.88 g sat fat, 1.66 g unsat fat, 66 mg chol, 169.3 mg sodium.

Cucumber Dressing

⅓ cup reduced-fat mayonnaise
   or salad dressing
1 teaspoon no-salt herbal
   seasoning
1 teaspoon chopped fresh dill
   or ⅓ teaspoon dried

¼ teaspoon pepper
⅓ cup lemon juice
1 cup puréed cucumber
1 small cucumber, pared and
   diced

Combine all the ingredients and chill at least 1 hour.

Yield: 2 cups.

Each tablespoon provides: about 10 cal, 0.5 g fat, no chol, 17 mg sodium.

South of the Border Curried Chicken with Rice and Jamaican Rum

Play rumba music while you enjoy this whole meal in a dish. Both onions and garlic tend to lower cholesterol levels; tomatoes provide lots of vitamin A, potassium, and iron; brown rice is a powerhouse of morale-boosting B vitamins and provides valuable rice bran, credited with lowering harmful cholesterol levels.

2 broiler-fryers (2½ to 3 pounds each), cut in serving-size pieces
1 cup finely chopped onions
2 cloves garlic, minced
¼ cup chopped green peppers
1½ cups canned tomatoes
½ teaspoon freshly ground pepper

2 teaspoons curry powder
½ teaspoon oregano
1 teaspoon no-salt herbal seasoning
5 cups low-sodium chicken broth, divided
3 tablespoons Jamaican rum
2 tablespoons paprika
1½ cups brown rice

Remove from the chickens all the visible fat and some of the fatty skin and render them in a heavy skillet. Remove the chicken cracklings and all but 2 tablespoons of chicken fat.

Sauté the onions, garlic, and green peppers in the skillet for about 10 minutes. Add the tomatoes, ground pepper, herbal seasoning, curry powder, oregano, and 2 cups of the broth. Cook over low heat for about 20 minutes. Add the rum and cook 10 minutes longer.

While the sauce is cooking, prepare the chickens and rice. Sprinkle the chicken with the paprika and broil until tender.

Bring the remaining broth to a boil. Stir in the rice. Cover and cook over low heat for 40 minutes or until tender. Watch carefully and add a little more water or broth if necessary.

Place the rice in a heavy saucepan or Dutch oven. Arrange the chicken over the rice. Pour the sauce over all. Cover and cook over low heat for 10 minutes.

Yield: 8 servings.

Each serving provides: 261 cal, 24 g pro, 1.5 g sat fat, 3.2 g unsat fat, 70 mg chol, 251 mg sodium.

Yorkshire Batter-Baked Chicken

The batter, made with oat bran, whole wheat flour, and wheat germ, contributes a pleasant crunch, lots of heart-healthy fiber and the whole family of B vitamins.

1 broiler-fryer (about 2½ to 3 pounds), cut in serving pieces

2 tablespoons oat bran (for coating)

2 tablespoons wheat germ or whole wheat flour (for coating)

1 teaspoon salt-free herbal seasoning (for coating)

½ teaspoon freshly ground pepper (for coating)

4 eggs

1½ cups low-sodium chicken broth

1½ cups whole wheat pastry flour (for batter)

1 teaspoon paprika

1 teaspoon sodium-free herbal seasoning (for batter)

¼ teaspoon pepper (for batter)

Cut from the chicken all the visible fat and some of the fatty skin and render them in a heavy skillet. Remove and reserve the chicken cracklings.

On waxed paper, combine the oat bran, wheat germ or whole wheat flour, and herbal seasoning for the coating. Coat the chicken and brown the pieces well in the fat in the skillet. Remove the chicken from the skillet but do not discard the pan drippings.

TO MAKE THE BATTER: In a medium-size bowl, beat the eggs until light. Stir in the chicken broth. Combine the flour, paprika, herbal seasoning, and pepper, and add to the egg mixture. Beat just until the batter is smooth. Stir in the pan drippings and the reserved cracklings.

Preheat the oven to 375°F. Coat a 13×9×2-inch baking dish with no-fat cooking spray and heat the dish in the oven.

Pour the batter into the heated baking dish and arrange the chicken pieces in the batter.

Bake for 45 minutes or until golden and puffy.

Yield: 6 servings.

Each serving provides: 270 cal, 24 g pro, 1.2 g sat fat, 2.2 g unsat fat, 162 mg chol, 133 mg sodium.

Left Bank Dijon Chicken

This is not mild-flavored, but it isn't tongue-stinging hot, either. You can safely serve it to family or friends of varying taste buds. They'll love it!

2 broiler-fryers (about 2½ to 3 pounds each), cut into serving-size pieces
¾ cup low-sodium chicken broth
¾ cup tarragon vinegar

3 tablespoons salt-free Dijon mustard
1 teaspoon salt-free herbal seasoning
½ teaspoon freshly ground pepper

Remove all visible fat and some of the fatty skin from the chicken and reserve for another use.

In a large bowl, combine the broth, vinegar, mustard, herbal seasoning, and pepper. Add the chicken and marinate at least 2 hours in the refrigerator, turning once.

Place the chicken pieces skin side down on the broiler rack. Broil 6 inches from the heat for 15 minutes. Turn and broil 20 to 30 minutes longer, basting frequently until the chicken is tender.

Yield: 8 servings.

Each serving provides: 131 cal, 21.5 g pro, 1.5 g sat fat, 2.5 g unsat fat, 70 mg chol, 109 mg sodium.

Chicken Tel Aviv

So simple to prepare and so good! Serve with thin spaghetti or couscous to mop up the delicious sauce.

1 broiler-fryer (2½ to 3 pounds), cut in serving-size pieces
1 cup tomato sauce with mushrooms (Rokeach, no salt added)
1 leek, thinly sliced (1 cup) or 1 cup chopped onions
1 can (3 or 4 ounces) chopped mushrooms
¼ cup chicken broth or water
2 tablespoons lemon juice

Remove all the visible fat from the chicken; reserve for another use. Arrange the chicken in a 13×9×2-inch baking dish.

In a medium-size bowl, combine the tomato sauce with mushrooms, leek or onions, chopped mushrooms, chicken broth or water, and lemon juice. Spoon over the chicken pieces.

Bake at 375°F for 1 hour or until the chicken is tender and nicely browned.

Yield: 4 servings.

Each serving provides: 180 cal, 21.6 g pro, 1.5 g sat fat, 2.5 g unsal fut, 70 mg chol, 198 mg sodium.

Chicken Sabra
with Bing Cherries and Brown Rice

Delightful to behold and delicious to eat. Definitely a celebration dish.

1 broiler-fryer (3½ to 4 pounds), cut in serving-size pieces
1 teaspoon no-salt herbal seasoning
1 teaspoon paprika
2 large onions, sliced
½ cup chicken stock

2 cups pitted bing cherries, fresh or frozen
1 tablespoon honey
2 tablespoons orange, apple, or apricot juice
1½ cups long-grain brown rice
4 cups water

Remove all the visible fat and some of the fatty skin and render it in a large, heavy skillet. Remove the chicken cracklings and all but 2 tablespoons of the chicken fat; reserve for another use.

Add the chicken pieces to the hot fat. Cook for about 5 minutes on each side to brown. Remove the chicken, and brown the onions in the skillet. Return the chicken to the skillet and add the chicken stock. Bring to a boil, then reduce the heat to low. Cover the skillet and simmer for 30 minutes or until the chicken is fork-tender.

While the chicken is simmering, combine the cherries, honey, and 2 tablespoons of fruit juice in a saucepan over very low heat.

Partially cook the rice by combining it with 4 cups of water in a large saucepan. Bring to a boil, then reduce the heat and simmer for 20 minutes. Drain the rice through a strainer, reserving the liquid.

Combine the pan drippings and 1 cup of the reserved rice water in a large, ovenproof casserole. Spreading it out evenly, put half the rice in the casserole. Add the chicken pieces, onions, and half the cherries. Arrange the rest of the rice on top of the mixture. Add the remaining cherries with their cooking liquid. Cover the casserole and simmer for 20 minutes or until the rice is tender.

Arrange half the rice on your prettiest serving platter. Arrange the chicken pieces and the onions on top of the bed of rice. Top the chicken with the cherries and half the remaining rice. Make an attractive border with the rest of the rice.

Yield: 6 servings.

Each serving provides: 327 cal, 22.6 g pro, 1 g sat fat, 2 g unsat fat, 70 mg chol, 66 mg sodium.

Canton Chicken with Almonds

Serve with bowls of hot brown rice and toasty oat bran crunch for a delicious meal that is high in fiber and nutrient-rich.

2 tablespoons chicken fat or olive oil (or 1 tablespoon of each)
1 teaspoon no-salt herbal seasoning
2 cups diced raw chicken
1 tablespoon reduced-sodium soy sauce
1 cup diced celery

½ cup canned mushrooms
1 cup cooked peas
1 cup hot chicken stock or boiling water
1 tablespoon arrowroot or cornstarch
¼ cup cold water
½ cup toasted whole almonds

Heat the chicken fat or olive oil in a large skillet or a wok. Add the seasoning and the chicken and sauté for about 3 minutes. Add the soy sauce and stir well. Add the celery, mushrooms, peas, and stock or water very slowly and stir well. Cover and cook for 4 minutes.

Mix the arrowroot or cornstarch with the cold water and add to the chicken mixture. Lower the heat and simmer until the gravy thickens. Remove from the heat and transfer to a serving plate. Sprinkle with toasted whole almonds.

Yield: 4 servings.

Each serving provides: 310 cal, 35.4 g pro, 3.38 g sat fat, 15 g unsat fat, 66 mg chol, 325 mg sodium.

Israeli Chicken Bake with Matzoh and Dill

Delicious any time, but especially welcome as a change from roast chicken for Passover.

2 cups cooked diced chicken
1 onion, finely chopped
6 eggs, beaten
3 tablespoons chopped parsley
3 teaspoons dried dill
1½ teaspoons no-salt herbal
    seasoning

½ teaspoon black pepper
3 squares matzoh, preferably
    whole wheat
2 cups chicken stock
3 teaspoons oil or chicken fat

In a large mixing bowl, combine the chicken, onion, eggs, parsley, dill, herbal seasoning, and pepper.

Pour 2 cups of chicken stock in a flat soup plate. Moisten the matzohs well in the chicken stock.

Preheat the oven to 400°F. Place one teaspoon of oil or chicken fat in a 9-inch-square baking dish and heat the fat in the preheating oven.

Lay one matzoh on the bottom of the baking dish and spread half of the chicken mixture over it. Cover with a second moistened matzoh, spread the remaining chicken mixture over this, and top with the third matzoh. Dribble another teaspoon of fat over the top and bake for 15 minutes. Add the remaining fat and bake until the top is browned—approximately 15 minutes.

Yield: 6 servings.

Each serving provides: 339 cal, 35 g pro, 4.2 g sat fat, 8.9 g unsat fat, 266 mg chol, 298 mg sodium.

Coke 'n' Chicken

What a combination! The following recipe is adapted from one that won top honors in a chicken recipe contest held in Israel. It sounded bizarre, so I wanted to try it. But I had no Coca-Cola, so I substituted unsweetened pineapple juice. For the ketchup, I substituted tomato sauce. I was amazed at how good it was. Then I tried the original Coca-Cola version. It was very tasty. For a once-in-a-while lark, here's the Coca-Cola version. For better nutritional value, try my revised version.

2 medium-size onions, chopped

½ cup Coca-Cola Classic or ½ cup unsweetened pineapple juice

¼ cup ketchup or ¼ cup tomato sauce

2 tablespoons vinegar, preferably balsamic

½ cup fruit juice-sweetened apricot conserves

2 tablespoons Worcestershire sauce

½ teaspoon chili powder

3 medium-size sweet potatoes, cut in ½-inch chunks

2 small chickens (about 2½ pounds each), cut in serving pieces

In a heavy saucepan, combine all ingredients except the chickens and the sweet potatoes. Bring to a boil, reduce the heat, and simmer, covered, for about 30 minutes, or until the sauce is thickened, while stirring occasionally.

Arrange the chicken pieces in an ovenproof casserole. Arrange the sweet potato chunks around the border of the dish. Pour the Worcestershire sauce over the chicken and over the sweet potatoes. Bake in a 350°F oven for 1 hour or until the chicken is tender.

Yield: 8 servings.

Each serving provides: 235 cal, 39 g pro, 2 g sat fat, 3.5 g unsat fat, 70 mg chol, 164 mg sodium.

Toasty Persian Chicken Balls

This is a great appetizer, small enough for the calorie-counter and hearty enough for the hungry bears. I like to keep a supply at the ready in the freezer. Unexpected company always marvels at how I whip them up so fast.

1 cup cooked chicken, boned
2 teaspoons chopped parsley
2 teaspoons oat bran
2 teaspoons minced onion

1 tablespoon curry powder
prepared mustard
1 egg, slightly beaten
2 teaspoons sesame seeds

In a chopping bowl or food processor, chop the chicken fine. Add the parsley, oat bran, onion, and curry powder, and process to blend the ingredients.

Add only enough mustard to make a moist paste. Shape into small balls, the size of a hickory nut, roll in the egg and then in the sesame seeds. Freeze or refrigerate for 1 hour or longer. Toast in a 450°F oven for 10 to 15 minutes.

Yield: Approximately 36 toasties.

Each toasty provides: 10 cal, 1 g pro, hardly a trace of fat, 2 mg chol, 8 mg sodium.

Moroccan Chicken Stew
with Olives and Avocado

Avocados and olives bring a powerhouse of fountain-of-youth nutrients to this fantastic dish. Don't limit this dish to special occasions; it makes every occasion special.

2 chickens (about 3 pounds each), cut in serving pieces, skin removed and reserved
1 large onion, chopped
2 cloves garlic, minced
½ cup orange juice
1 teaspoon herbal seasoning
⅛ teaspoon freshly ground pepper
1 tablespoon fresh tarragon or ½ teaspoon dried
1 lemon, washed and thinly sliced
¼ cup fresh parsley, chopped
1 cup pitted black olives
1 avocado, peeled, cubed, and tossed in orange juice

Remove all visible fat from the chicken. Cut the chicken skin in smallish pieces. In a large, heavy skillet, render the fat and skin until the cracklings are brown and crisp. If you get more than 2 tablespoons of fat, remove it along with the cracklings and reserve for another use. If you get less than 2 tablespoons, add a little olive oil or canola oil to make up the difference.

Add the cut-up chicken to the skillet and brown on all sides. Add the onion, garlic, orange juice, herbal seasoning, pepper, and lemon. Cook for 15 minutes. Stir in the parsley and olives. Cover and cook over moderate heat for about 25 minutes or until the chicken is cooked.

Stir occasionally and add water or chicken broth if it seems dry.

Remove the chicken to a serving dish and spoon the olive mixture over it. Top with the cubed avocado.

Yield: 8 servings.

Each serving provides: 215 cal, 31.5 g pro, 3.5 g sat fat, 4.5 g unsat fat, 70 mg chol, 135 mg sodium.

Farfel Chicken Casserole

This is a great dish for Passover but can be enjoyed any time you want to make a little leftover chicken go a long, long way. It can be made with macaroni for non-Passover use.

1 to 2 teaspoons chicken fat or peanut oil
1 large onion, diced
1 cup chicken soup or stock
1 cup vegetable juice, stock, or water
2 cups cut-up cooked chicken
2 cups cooked sliced carrots or other cooked vegetables
1 cup diced celery
1½ cups matzoh farfel (available at Jewish delicatessens), or break whole wheat matzohs into pieces no larger than a thumbnail
pepper and paprika

In a large, heavy saucepan, heat the chicken fat or peanut oil. Add the onion and sauté until transparent but not brown. Add the chicken soup or stock and the vegetable juice, stock, or water. Cook for about 5 minutes to make a sauce.

In a 2-quart casserole, arrange the chicken, vegetables, matzoh farfel, and the sauce in alternate layers. Season to taste with pepper and paprika. Cover and bake in a preheated 350°F oven for about 30 minutes.

Yield: 6 servings.

Each serving provides: 154 cal, 16 g pro, 1.2 g sat fat, 3 g unsat fat, 66 mg chol, 204 mg sodium.

11
TURKEY

Turkey and Almond Salad
Chinese Turkey Salad
Sparkling Turkey Salad
Celebration Turkey Puff Pie
Turkey Filling
Turkey Hash
Turkey Chow Mein
Polynesian Turkey
Turkey and Broccoli Frittata

You can't mention Thanksgiving without evoking the tantalizing aroma of a succulent turkey. And when you think of turkey, you recall the holiday nostalgia of family reunions around the Thanksgiving table.

Thanksgiving comes but once a year. But there's no reason at all why we can't enjoy turkey much more frequently and be thankful each time it shows up on the menu. The big gobbler just happens to be a very good nutritional buy—and the answer to the prayers of the epicurean waistline-watcher. It is extremely low in fat and very high in protein.

Turkey comes in sizes that might be too large for your own family. But when you consider that turkey freezes well and can then be incorporated into a great variety of fantastic dishes, your investment in the big bird is more than justified.

Turkey is high in essential fatty acids, yet one of the lowest of all meats in calories. It is also an excellent source of riboflavin (B_2), which is especially important to your skin and eyes, and niacin, which is necessary to a host of mental functions and to the reduction of high cholesterol levels.

So turkey on the menu does help to keep those faces glowing, eyes sparkling, and the conversation bright and merry. (All the time you thought it was your great cooking!) Not that cooking it right doesn't help. It sure does. So here are some hints:

If you can get a fresh turkey from someone you know who raises them naturally, you're in luck. But fresh turkeys are hard to come by, so you will probably settle for a frozen one.

Before you cook it, thaw it in the refrigerator. A large bird takes two to four days, half that time for a small bird. If, when you are ready to cook it, the turkey is not completely thawed, then put it under cold running water to finish the job.

Never let the thawed bird stand around at room temperature. It should go from freezer to refrigerator to sink to oven. Prepare the stuffing ahead of time but never stuff the bird until it's ready for the oven.

COOKING THE BIG BIRD

Start the turkey early enough in the day so you can roast it in a slow oven—325°F. Slow oven roasting preserves more moisture and juices and does the least violence to the many nutrients in the turkey meat. (Figure on 20 minutes for every pound.) Plan your roasting time so that the turkey will be done about a half hour before its grand entrance. The rest period before curtain time makes carving easy and gives you time to prepare the gravy.

If you plan to stuff the bird, fill it loosely with the stuffing of your choice. Remember, it will expand. Don't forget to stuff the neck cavity, too. An average-size turkey (up to 12 pounds) will take 2 to 3 quarts of stuffing. It's a good idea to make extra stuffing and bake it separately in a casserole or as individual servings in muffin tins, to be used at a later meal when the turkey comes back for an encore.

After stuffing the bird, close the openings with skewers or sew with strong white thread, and truss securely.

Preheat the oven to 325°F.

To put a becoming blush on your turkey, try this method, which always gets a standing ovation at our house.

In a small bowl, combine these ingredients: several cloves of crushed garlic; the juice of 2 lemons; 4 tablespoons of tomato paste; and 1 teaspoon each of poultry seasoning or sage, thyme, marjoram, herbal seasoning, and paprika. These amounts are for a 10-pound turkey, so judge accordingly.

Rub the turkey inside and outside with this mixture, then place it, breast side up, on a rack in a roaster. Roast, uncovered, basting about every half hour with the pan drippings. If the turkey browns too quickly while roasting, tent it with parchment paper or aluminum foil.

The best way to determine doneness is to insert a thermometer in the thigh muscle. It should register 185°F. Another test for doneness is to pierce the thigh with the tip of a small, sharp knife. The juices should be clear. If the juices are tinged with pink, roast for about 10 minutes more. When it tests done, transfer to a heated platter and let it rest before carving.

Meanwhile, make the gravy. Pour off all but 2 tablespoons of fat from the roasting pan. Stir about 2 tablespoons of arrowroot, cornstarch, or whole wheat flour into the pan. When it is absorbed, add a cup of hot water or stock. Heat to a boil, stirring constantly with a wire whisk, and incorporate into the liquid all the flavorful, brown crusty pieces on the bottom and sides of the pan. Season to taste, and pour into a heated gravy boat.

ROASTING WITHOUT BASTING

This is a carefree method of achieving luscious juiciness. Prepare the turkey the same as for oven roasting. Moisten a large sheet of parchment paper (available at some department stores and cookware or specialty shops). For large birds, use two widths. Place the turkey breast side up in the middle of the parchment. Bring the long ends up over the breast and overlap 3 inches. Close open ends by folding up the parchment paper to prevent drippings from running into the pan. Now wrap the whole thing in foil in the same manner to keep the parchment intact. The foil does not come in contact with the bird.

Place the wrapped turkey, breast side up, in a roasting pan. No rack is needed. An hour before you expect the bird to be done, fold back the parchment and foil completely to bring a becoming blush and some crispness to the skin. Give it the thermometer or thigh test for doneness. When the juices run clear, your bird is ready for some of the most appreciative exclamations of gustatorial delight that will ever pleasure your soul.

ONCE IS NOT ENOUGH

The turkey was scrumptious, the family loved it. But you still have half a bird left. How shall you fix it? Let me count the ways. There's hash, stew, chop suey, casseroles, stir-fry dishes with vegetables, scrapple, pancakes, crepes, sandwiches, and salads, and whatever else your own creative juices come up with.

(These recipes for leftover turkey can be used for any cooked poultry, whether chicken, capon, goose, duck, or guinea hen.)

SALADS

You can enjoy a turkey salad the day after Thanksgiving or a month after the holiday. Simply pack one cup of cut-up turkey in a carton and freeze. You will always have workable amounts to use in salads, casseroles, to fill crepes, or whatever.

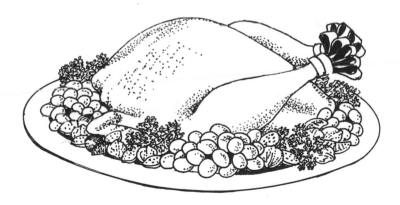

Turkey and Almond Salad

Easy to prepare, light, and yet festive. It's a nice change from the rather heavy Thanksgiving dinner and is most welcome when served the day after the holiday.

2 cups diced cooked turkey
½ cup chopped celery
½ cup slivered or chopped
    almonds, lightly roasted

1 cup presoaked raisins;
    reserve the liquid
⅓ cup reduced-fat mayonnaise
    lettuce

In a glass bowl, combine the turkey, celery, presoaked raisins, and almonds.

In a small dish, mix together ⅓ cup raisin liquid and ⅓ cup mayonnaise. Stir into the turkey mixture. Serve on a bed of dark green lettuce.

Yield: 6 servings.

Each serving provides: 276 cal, 17 g pro, 2.1 g sat fat, 9.2 g unsat fat, 66 mg chol, 182 mg sodium.

Chinese Turkey Salad

The same turkey has an entirely different flavor when you go Oriental and serve Chinese turkey salad.

1 cup cooked turkey
1½ teaspoons Tamari soy sauce
½ cup slivered bamboo shoots
    (optional)
1 cup coarsely shredded
    lettuce or Chinese
    cabbage
3 red radishes, thinly sliced

¼ cup coarsely chopped
    walnuts
1 cup bean sprouts
2 tablespoons olive oil
1½ tablespoons vinegar,
    preferably rice or balsamic
¼ teaspoon powdered ginger
    lettuce

Cut the turkey into matchstick strips and marinate in the soy sauce for 20 minutes.

In a glass bowl, combine the turkey, bamboo shoots if you're using them, lettuce or cabbage, radishes, walnuts, and sprouts. Toss lightly.

In a small dish, mix together the oil, vinegar, and ginger until well blended. Pour over the salad, tossing lightly to coat the mixture. Serve on a bed of dark green lettuce.

Yield: 4 servings.

Each serving provides: 151 cal, 17 g pro, 3 g fat, 10.3 g unsat fat, 78 mg chol, 41 mg sodium.

Sparkling Turkey Salad

This is a lovely make-ahead main dish for a special occasion, buffet-bring-a-dish party, luncheon, or festive family dinner.

2½ cups diced cold turkey
1 cup white seedless grapes
½ cup slivered or chopped
   almonds, lightly toasted
2 tablespoons minced parsley
1 stalk celery, finely chopped
1½ tablespoons gelatin

4 tablespoons cold water
½ cup chicken or turkey stock
¾ cup reduced-calorie mayonnaise or salad dressing
¼ cup no-salt-added Dijon
   mustard
salad greens

Combine the turkey, grapes, almonds, parsley, and celery.

In a small bowl, soak the gelatin in cold water for 5 minutes, then dissolve in boiling stock.

Combine the mayonnaise and mustard. Add the gelatin stock to the mayonnaise mixture and stir until the mixture begins to thicken. Fold in the turkey mixture. Pack in 1 large mold or in 8 individual molds. Unmold on a bed of salad greens.

Yield: 8 servings.

Each serving provides: 239 cal, 18 g pro, 1.3 g sat fat, 8.1 g unsat fat, 135 mg chol, 239 mg sodium.

Variation: Line each mold with slices of hard-cooked egg for a lovely effect.

Celebration Turkey Puff Pie

A great dish for big events, a delight to the eye and the palate. Picture a classic cream puff dough flavored with mustard and sesame seeds, filled with turkey and sautéed mushrooms, and topped with crunchy marbles of puffery.

¾ cup water
6 tablespoons tahini (sesame butter)
¾ cup whole wheat flour
3 eggs

1 teaspoon herbal seasoning
½ teaspoon dry mustard
turkey filling (recipe follows)

In a heavy saucepan, bring the water and tahini to a boil. Add the flour all at once. Cook, beating hard with a wooden spoon, until the ingredients are well blended and the mixture leaves the sides of the pan (about 30 seconds).

Remove the pan from the heat and add the eggs, one at a time, beating well after each addition. Mix in the herbal seasoning and mustard.

Coat a 9-inch pie pan with nonstick baking spray. Using ⅔ of the dough, line the bottom and sides of pan. (The dough will be sticky; moisten your fingers or use the back of a spoon to spread.)

Spoon the filling into the crust. Using the remaining dough, form teaspoon-size puffs around the top of the filling. Bake at 375°F for 40 to 45 minutes, until puffed and well browned. Serve piping hot.

Turkey Filling

1 onion, diced
1 cup sliced mushrooms
1 tablespoon chicken fat or
  olive oil

1 tablespoon whole wheat
  flour
½ cup chicken or turkey stock
2 cups cooked turkey, diced

In a large, heavy skillet, sauté the onion and mushrooms in the fat or olive oil. Add the flour and blend. Cook about 1 minute. Add the stock and cook until thickened, about 4 minutes. Stir in the turkey and season to taste. Heat through, then place it in the pie crust. **Yield:** 6 servings.

Each serving provides: 235 cal, 22 g pro, 2.6 g sat fat, 7.1 g unsat fat, 135 mg chol, 232 mg sodium.

Turkey Hash

Once the standby on washday because it is so easy to prepare, but you can serve it with pride any day of the week. Topped with a poached egg, it makes a great breakfast or brunch dish.

1 medium onion, minced
½ green or red pepper, diced
2 tablespoons chicken or
  turkey fat, or olive oil
2 cups cooked diced turkey
  meat
2 cups cooked potatoes, diced,
  or brown rice

¼ cup apple sauce
1 tablespoon minced parsley
1 teaspoon herbal seasoning
⅛ teaspoon freshly ground
  pepper
½ teaspoon poultry seasoning
  or sage
4 poached eggs (optional)

In a large, heavy skillet, stir-fry the onion and pepper in the turkey fat or olive oil, until the onion is golden. Add the remaining ingredients except the eggs. Press down with a spatula and cook, uncovered, without stirring, about 10 minutes, or until a brown crust forms on the bottom. Turn and brown the flip side for about 10 minutes.

Top each serving with a poached egg if you choose.

Yield: 4 servings.

Each serving provides: 272 cal, 28 g pro, 2.7 g sat fat, 8.6 g unsat fat, 70 mg chol, 98 mg sodium.

Each serving topped with a poached egg provides: 350 cal, 34 g pro, 4.6 g sat fat, 11.5 g unsat fat, 320 mg chol, 157 mg sodium.

Turkey Chow Mein

This hearty, nutritious meal, cooked quickly in a wok, can be served on brown rice, Chinese crispy noodles, or soft cellophane noodles.

1 cup sliced mushrooms
2 onions, minced
3 stalks celery, diced
2 tablespoons chicken or
    turkey fat or olive oil
2 cups chicken or turkey broth
2 tablespoons Tamari soy
    sauce
2 tablespoons arrowroot or
    cornstarch

¼ cup cold water
½ teaspoon herbal seasoning
3 cups cooked turkey, cut in
    bite-size pieces
1½ cups mung bean sprouts
1 cup water chestnuts,
    drained, or Jerusalem
    artichokes, sliced thin
½ cup almonds or cashews,
    lightly roasted

In a heavy skillet or wok, stir-fry the onions, celery, and mushrooms in the fat or olive oil for about 8 minutes or until golden brown. Add the broth and soy sauce. Turn the heat to low, cover, and simmer for about 8 minutes.

Dissolve the arrowroot or cornstarch in cold water, then add to the pot. Continue to cook, stirring, until the liquid is thickened. Lower the heat and add the turkey, bean sprouts, and water chestnuts or Jerusalem artichokes. Continue to heat and stir for about 5 minutes.

Stir in the almonds or cashews and serve over hot brown rice or noodles.

Yield: 6 servings.

Each serving provides: 301.5 cal, 7 g pro, 2.3 g sat fat, 12 g unsat fat, 70 mg chol, 240 mg sodium.

Polynesian Turkey

A sweet and sour dish that is easy to prepare and always makes a hit. Serve over brown rice or as a topping for baked potatoes.

1 can (20 ounces) pineapple chunks packed without added sweetener
¼ cup apple cider vinegar
2 tablespoons honey
2 tablespoons arrowroot or cornstarch

1 tablespoon Tamari soy sauce
2½ cups cooked turkey, diced
1 green pepper cut into 1½-inch strips
1 small onion, thinly sliced
hot cooked brown rice or baked potatoes

Drain the pineapple, reserving the juice. Combine one cup of the pineapple juice with the vinegar, honey, arrowroot or cornstarch, and soy sauce. Cook over low heat until thickened, stirring constantly. Remove from the heat and add the turkey. Let stand, covered, for 10 minutes.

Place the green pepper strips in a little boiling water and cover. Let stand for 5 minutes. Drain well. Add the green pepper, onion, and pineapple chunks to the turkey mixture and heat. Season to taste.

Yield: 6 servings.

Each serving with ½ cup brown rice or 1 medium-size baked potato provides: approximately 179 cal, 18 g pro, 1.26 g sat fat, 2.52 g unsat fat, 66 mg chol, 162.5 mg sodium.

Turkey and Broccoli Frittata

This is an adaptation of an omelet we very much enjoyed in Italy. Uncommonly good for a weekend family breakfast, lunch, or brunch, or for a patio dinner. Served this way, even President Bush would eat his broccoli and love it.

3 tablespoons olive oil, chicken fat, or a combination of both
1 medium-size yellow onion, finely chopped
1 large clove garlic, minced
¾ cup cooked turkey, chopped
2 cups broccoli florets, chopped

½ cup cooked brown rice or pasta (optional)
6 eggs
2 teaspoons chopped fresh oregano or ½ teaspoon dried
½ teaspoon red pepper flakes, crushed

Heat 2 tablespoons of the olive oil or chicken fat in a heavy, 10-inch skillet. Add the onion and sauté, stirring, until the onion is wilted and golden—about 6 minutes. Add the garlic and turkey and cook, stirring, for about 4 minutes. Stir in the broccoli and rice or pasta, if you're using it, and toss. Remove from the heat and set aside.

In a large bowl, food processor, or mixing machine, whisk the eggs until they are frothy. Add the turkey mixture and the oregano to the eggs.

Over moderate heat, add the remaining oil or fat to the skillet. Add the egg mixture, reduce the heat to low, and cook until the eggs are firm and brown on the underside—about 8 to 10 minutes. Sprinkle the red pepper flakes over the top, then run it under the broiler for about 4 minutes. Cut in wedges and serve from the skillet.

Yield: 6 servings.

Each serving provides: 210 cal, 15 g pro, 3.1 g sat fat, 8.1 g unsat fat, 316 mg chol, 100 mg sodium.

12

MARVELOUS CHICKEN LIVER DISHES

Curried Chicken Livers with Apples
Chicken Liver Pâté with Toasted Almonds
Oriental-Style Chicken Livers and Rice
Chopped Chicken Liver
Chicken Livers and Spinach with Pistachios
Chicken Liver Soufflé
Stewed Chicken Livers, Gizzards, and Hearts
Grilled Chicken Livers with Mushrooms

If you've been enjoying chicken frequently, you probably have a goodly store of chicken livers in the freezer. Now's your chance to put them to good use and enhance the menu for a lovely family meal or for a very special occasion. Liver is the most nutritious of meats, especially rich in iron, vitamin A, and the B vitamins, including folic acid, which is important to everyone's health but especially important to women contemplating pregnancy. Well-documented research reveals that a deficiency of folic acid in the mother is responsible for such birth defects as spina bifida and cleft palate.

True, liver is high in cholesterol, but it has practically no saturated fat. Research points to saturated fat as the prime instigator of high cholesterol levels.

If, however, your doctor has restricted your cholesterol intake, enjoy chicken livers once in a while and limit your intake of other sources of high cholesterol foods on those occasions.

Curried Chicken Livers with Apples

Chicken livers go with chicken fat like love and marriage. If you don't have any chicken fat, use chicken broth.

1 pound chicken livers
1 teaspoon chicken fat (no substitutes)
½ cup chopped onions
¼ teaspoon curry powder
1 unpeeled apple (preferably Granny Smith), coarsely chopped
¼ cup raisins

2 tablespoons marsala wine
1 teaspoon arrowroot or cornstarch
2 tablespoons water
1 teaspoon no-salt herbal seasoning
¼ teaspoon freshly grated pepper

Cut the livers in halves and broil them 6 inches from the source of heat for 5 minutes on each side.

Heat the chicken fat in a heavy skillet. Add the onions, and sauté till tender. Stir in the chicken livers and curry powder. Add the apple and raisins, cover, and simmer for 10 minutes. Stir in the wine. Dissolve the arrowroot or cornstarch in the water and add to the mixture. Heat until slightly thickened. Add the seasonings.

Serve with hot cooked brown or wild rice, or a mixture of both. Garnish with thin apple slices and parsley or watercress.

Yield: 5 servings.

Each serving provides: 160 cal, 24 g pro, 1 g sat fat, 2 g unsat fat, 200 mg chol, 100 mg sodium.

Chicken Liver Pâté with Toasted Almonds

1 tablespoon chicken fat
3 tablespoons chopped onion
½ pound chicken livers
2 tablespoons vermouth
1 hard-cooked egg
1 teaspoon herbal seasoning

¼ teaspoon freshly ground
   pepper
dash of nutmeg
½ cup toasted almonds,
   chopped

In a small skillet, heat the fat and sauté the onion. Set aside.

Broil the chicken livers for 5 minutes on each side.

Whir together in a food processor or chop in a wooden bowl the sautéed onions, livers, vermouth, egg, herbal seasoning, pepper, and nutmeg. Add a little chicken broth if necessary to make the pâté smoother. Fold in the chopped almonds. Refrigerate until ready to serve.

Yield: 2½ cups.

Each ¼-cup serving provides: 90 cal, 5 g pro, 1.8 g sat fat, 3.2 g unsat fat, 105 mg chol, 13 mg sodium.

Variation: Instead of chopped almonds, fold in chopped chicken cracklings.

Oriental-Style Chicken Livers and Rice

1 cup uncooked brown rice
2½ cups chicken broth
1 pound chicken livers, cut in
   halves
2 tablespoons minced onion
2 tablespoons chopped green
   pepper

2 tablespoons chicken fat or
   olive oil, or a mixture
2 tablespoons reduced-sodium
   soy sauce
¼ teaspoon ground ginger

In a large saucepan, combine the rice and chicken broth. Bring to a boil, cover, and simmer for 35 minutes or until the liquid is absorbed and the rice is tender.

Broil the chicken livers for 3 minutes on each side.

In a heavy skillet, heat the chicken fat or olive oil. Brown the chicken livers, onion, and pepper. Stir in the soy sauce and ginger.

Spoon the rice onto a serving platter. Place the chicken livers in the center.

Yield: 4 servings.

Each serving provides: 388 cal, 29 g pro, 3.9 g sat fat, 7 g unsat fat, 402 mg chol, 610 mg sodium.

Chopped Chicken Liver

This is the kind that Mamma used to make. For a special taste of nostalgia, serve it with grated white radish.

1 to 2 tablespoons chicken fat	½ cup chicken cracklings
¾ pound chicken livers (about 7 livers)	(grieben)
	1 large romaine leaf
1 large onion, chopped fine	1 teaspoon herbal seasoning
½ cup diced celery (optional)	½ teaspoon freshly ground
1 hard-cooked egg	pepper, or to taste

In a large, heavy skillet, heat the fat and add the livers and onion, and the celery if you're using it. Sauté until the livers are firm but not overdone.

Combine the contents of the skillet with the hard-cooked egg, cracklings, and the romaine leaf. Put everything through a food chopper, or chop in a wooden bowl to a fine consistency but a slightly coarse texture. Add seasonings to taste. Shape the mixture into a neat mound and refrigerate. Serve cold, garnished with a sprig of parsley.

Yield: About 3 cups.

Each ¼-cup serving provides: 90 cal, 5 g pro, 1 g sat fat, 1.5 g unsat fat, 109 mg chol, 60 mg sodium.

Chicken Livers and Spinach with Pistachios

This dish is a powerhouse of antifatigue iron, folic acid, and B_{12}, plus a big bunch of vitamin A, which perks up the immune system and has been shown to increase resistance to malignancies. Serve it with fiber-rich brown rice and apple sauce.

1 pound spinach, trimmed and washed	1 cup chicken broth
1 pound chicken livers	3 tablespoons shelled and chopped pistachios

In a dry saucepan, cook the spinach over medium heat for 2 minutes or just until wilted. Remove and leave to cool.

Broil the chicken livers for 2 minutes on each side. Mince the chicken livers with a knife or poultry shears.

Chop the cooked spinach and combine it with the chicken livers. Moisten with the chicken broth. Pack this combination into a baking dish greased with a little oil or sprayed with no-stick baking spray. Top with the chopped pistachios and bake in a preheated 350°F oven for about 30 minutes.

Yield: 4 servings.

Each serving provides: 185 cal, 28 g pro, 1.5 g sat fat, 2.5 g unsat fat, 250 mg chol, 92 mg sodium.

Chicken Liver Soufflé

2 tablespoons plus 1 teaspoon
  chicken fat or olive oil
1 small onion, minced
3 tablespoons whole wheat
  flour
3 tablespoons oat bran
¼ teaspoon freshly ground
  pepper

¾ cup chicken broth
5 chicken livers
2 cloves garlic, minced
1 teaspoon finely minced fresh
  sage
3 tablespoons finely minced
  fresh parsley
4 eggs, separated

In a small skillet, heat 1 teaspoon chicken fat or olive oil. Add the onion and sauté until it is wilted and golden, about 8 minutes.

In a 2-quart saucepan, heat 2 tablespoons of fat. Add the flour, oat bran, and pepper, and stir with a wire whisk, cooking until bubbly but not brown. Whisk in the chicken broth gradually and cook slowly, stirring constantly until very thick, about 5 minutes. Remove from the heat and add the sautéed onions. Set aside to cool.

Broil the livers for 2 minutes on each side. In a food processor, food mill, or wooden bowl, blend the livers, garlic, sage, and parsley until smooth. Add this mixture to the sauce, then add the beaten egg yolks.

Coat a 2½-inch-deep soufflé dish with nonstick baking spray. Preheat the oven to 325°F.

In a medium-size bowl, beat the egg whites until stiff peaks form. Fold the whites into the liver mixture carefully. Spoon into the prepared soufflé dish and bake in the heated oven for 50 minutes or until a cake tester inserted in the center comes out clean. Serve at once before it deflates.

Yield: 6 servings.
Each serving provides: 151 cal, 10 g pro, 4 g sat fat, 5 g unsat fat, 215 mg chol, 200 mg sodium.

Stewed Chicken Livers, Gizzards, and Hearts

A hearty, warming, nourishing dish. Serve with fiber-rich barley or buckwheat groats (kasha).

2 cups chicken stock
½ cup coarsely chopped onions
1 bay leaf
¼ teaspoon freshly ground
    pepper
¼ pound chicken hearts
    (optional)
½ pound chicken gizzards, cut
    in half
1 pound chicken livers, cut in
    bite-size pieces
6 tablespoons oat bran, for
    dredging

2 tablespoons chicken fat or
    olive oil
2 cloves garlic, finely minced
1 cup thinly sliced mushrooms
3 stalks celery, chopped
3 carrots, finely chopped
1 tablespoon fresh basil,
    minced
1 tablespoon fresh thyme
    leaves

In a large, heavy pot, combine the chicken stock, onions, bay leaf, pepper, chicken gizzards, and chicken hearts, if you're using them. Bring to a boil, cover, and simmer for 45 minutes or until the gizzards are tender. Remove and discard the bay leaf. With a slotted spoon, lift out the gizzards and hearts. Reserve the stock.

Cut the livers in halves, then broil them 2 minutes on each side.

Dredge the livers in the oat bran. In a large skillet, heat the chicken fat or olive oil. Add the livers and sauté for 1 minute on each side. Lift out with a slotted spoon and reserve.

In the same skillet, add the garlic and mushrooms and stir for about 2 minutes over medium heat. Stir in the celery and carrots and cook for 2 more minutes. Add the reserved stock, gizzards, and hearts to the vegetables. Bring to a boil, cover, lower the heat, and simmer for about 12 minutes. Add the reserved livers and herbs and heat, stirring occasionally until the sauce is thickened—about 5 minutes. **Yield:** 6 servings.

Each serving provides: 204 cal, 22.2 g pro, 3 g sat fat, 4 g unsat fat, 319 mg chol, 210 mg sodium.

Grilled Chicken Livers with Mushrooms

A tender, crunchy, epicurean delight—it beats hot dogs for an out-door cookout.

1 pound chicken livers
1 tablespoon chicken fat or
   olive oil
¼ cup dry white wine
½ cup crushed oat bran crunch
   or your favorite high-
   fiber dry cereal

¼ teaspoon onion powder
¼ teaspoon dried oregano
8 medium-size mushrooms,
   halved, or 16 small
   mushrooms
8 cherry tomatoes

Cut the chicken livers in halves. Combine 1 tablespoon of chicken fat or olive oil and wine in a medium-size bowl and add the chicken livers. Marinate for 30 minutes, refrigerated.

On waxed paper, combine the cereal crumbs, onion powder, and oregano. Drain the chicken livers, reserving the marinade, and roll in the crumb mixture.

Thread the livers, mushrooms, and tomatoes alternately on 4 skewers. Brush with the reserved marinade.

Grill 15 minutes, turning once or until the livers are slightly browned.

Yield: 4 servings.

Each serving provides: 191 cal, 24 g pro, 2 g sat fat, 3 g unsat fat, 402 mg chol, 82 mg sodium.

13

SPEEDY STIR-FRY DISHES

Skinny Ginger Garlic Chicken
Israeli-Style Chicken Curry
Chicken Chow Mein
Orange Chicken and Bean Stir-fry
Chicken Chop Suey with Brandy Sauce

Stir-fry dishes can be very low in calories, highly nutritious, and exciting to make. A stir-fry always gets my creative juices flowing. There are so many different vegetables, grains, nuts, or seeds that can be added to a stir-fry, so many different herbs and condiments to mellow or sharpen flavors, so many nutritional dynamos you can add (or conceal, if you have a typically recalcitrant family), such as oat bran, rice bran, oatmeal, and all the veggies your family members think they don't like.

If you're on a tight schedule and must get dinner on the table in 15 minutes, prepare the vegetables when you do have time, blanche and freeze them in family-size packets, or use frozen vegetables.

Stir-fry dishes are quite flexible. They may be made from freshly cooked or leftover cooked poultry.

Another stir-fry virtue: a wonderful opportunity to use up all the odds and ends cluttering the refrigerator.

Skinny Ginger Garlic Chicken

Mushrooms and peppers are low-calorie pepper-uppers in this flavorful quick-and-easy dish.

1 chicken breast, boned and
    skinned (reserve the
    skin)
1 clove garlic, minced
1 slice ginger, minced
1 large red pepper, cut in
    wedges and sliced
1 large green or yellow
    pepper, cut in wedges
    and sliced

12 mushrooms, cleaned and
    sliced
4 water chestnuts, sliced
1 cup chicken broth
2 tablespoons reduced-sodium
    soy sauce
3 tablespoons sherry
½ teaspoon honey
2 cups cooked brown rice

Cut the breast in thin slices. Cut the skin in smallish pieces and render it in a heavy skillet or a wok. Remove the golden cracklings and reserve for another use. If the remaining fat is less than 2 tablespoons, add a little olive oil.

In the heated fat, lightly sauté the garlic and ginger for about a minute. Stir in the sliced chicken and cook for another minute. Add the peppers, mushrooms, and water chestnuts and cook until the chicken is cooked through.

Add the chicken broth, soy sauce, sherry, and honey and heat to combine the flavors. Serve over the brown rice or as a topping for baked potatoes.

Yield: 4 servings.

Each serving with ½ cup of brown rice provides: 177 cal, 13.5 g pro, 1.5 g sat fat, 3.12 g unsat fat, 66 mg chol, 328 mg sodium.

Israeli-Style Chicken Curry

Intensify the Israeli experience and serve with a crisp potato kugel and pineapple cole slaw.

2 whole chicken breasts, boned
    and skinned (reserve
    the skin)
2 teaspoons dry sherry
2 teaspoons arrowroot or
    cornstarch

1 clove garlic, crushed
1 teaspoon curry powder
1 teaspoon herbal seasoning
1 cup Chinese pea pods
1 tomato, cut in 8 wedges
¼ cup chicken broth

Cut the chicken breasts into strips about ½ inch wide. Marinate in the sherry mixed with the arrowroot or cornstarch for 30 minutes or longer.

Render the chicken skin to make chicken fat. Retain 2 teaspoons of the fat, or use 2 teaspoons of olive oil.

In a large, heavy skillet or a wok, heat the fat and brown the garlic. Add the chicken and cook quickly until it turns white. Sprinkle with the curry powder and herbal seasoning.

Remove the chicken from the pan. In the same pan stir-fry the pea pods and tomatoes until heated through. Return the chicken to the pan with the vegetables. Add the chicken broth and cook until heated through.

Yield: 4 servings.

Each serving provides: 154 cal, 20.2 g pro, 0.5 g sat fat, 1.56 g unsat fat, 33 mg chol, 185 mg sodium.

Chicken Chow Mein

Serve with brown rice. Pass the Chinese noodles and the chopsticks.

2 tablespoons olive oil or
   chicken fat or a
   combination
3 cups cooked chicken, cut in
   bite-size pieces
3 cups onions, sliced and then
   cut in half-moons
3 cups celery, sliced diagonally

3 cups chicken broth
2 cups bean sprouts
2 tablespoons arrowroot or
   cornstarch
2 tablespoons water
2 teaspoons reduced-sodium
   soy sauce
1 teaspoon honey

In a large skillet or a wok, heat the fat. Add the cut-up chicken. Sear it quickly without browning. Add the onions, and sauté for 3 minutes. Add the celery and chicken broth. Cook for 5 minutes or until the celery is slightly softened. Add the bean sprouts. Mix thoroughly and bring to a boil. Combine the arrowroot or cornstarch, water, soy sauce, and honey. Add to the chicken mixture. Cook 5 more minutes or until the sauce is slightly thickened.

Yield: 6 servings.

Each serving provides: 211 cal, 37 g pro, 1.2 g sat fat, 4.3 g unsat fat, 66 mg chol, 240 mg sodium.

Orange Chicken and Bean Stir-fry

Beans provide not only incomparable flavor, they are also rich in water-soluble fiber, the kind that has been shown to lower high cholesterol levels. In addition, they are rich in blood-building iron. The vitamin C in the orange helps you to absorb the iron in the beans and in the chicken.

2 chicken breasts, boned and skinned (reserve skin)
½ cup orange juice
1½ teaspoons chili powder
1½ teaspoons arrowroot or cornstarch
1 teaspoon herbal seasoning
2 medium green peppers, cut in ¼-inch pieces

1 medium yellow onion, cut in ¼-inch slices
2 cups cooked or canned red kidney beans, drained
2 medium tomatoes, cut in 8 wedges each

Cut the breasts crosswise in ⅛-inch slices.

In a shallow bowl, combine the orange juice, chili powder, arrowroot or cornstarch, and herbal seasoning. Add the chicken, stirring to mix. Set aside.

In a large skillet or a wok, render the skin of the chicken. Remove the cracklings and reserve. If you get less than 2 tablespoons of fat, add enough oil to make up the difference. Heat the fat to a high temperature, then add the peppers and onion and stir-fry about 4 minutes or just until the vegetables are crisp-tender.

Remove the vegetables and add the chicken to the drippings in the same skillet, but reserve the orange juice mixture.

Cook the chicken, stirring constantly, for about 5 minutes or until golden. Add the reserved orange mixture, sautéed onions and peppers, kidney beans, and tomato wedges. Cook, stirring until heated through.

Yield: 6 servings.

Each serving provides: 228 cal, 23 g pro, 2.5 g sat fat, 4 g unsat fat, 70 mg chol, 60 mg sodium.

Chicken Chop Suey with Brandy Sauce

Although this recipe calls for raw chicken, it can also be made from previously cooked chicken. It's delicious either way. The vegetables provide heart-healthy magnesium and potassium as well as beta-carotene, which has been shown to retard the development of carcinomas.

2 tablespoons olive, peanut, or canola oil
2 cups raw chicken, cut in 1-inch pieces
1 cup chicken broth
1 cup celery, cut in 1-inch chunks
12 water chestnuts, sliced (available in cans, or fresh at Oriental stores)

1 cup sliced, fresh mushrooms
1 cup sliced bamboo shoots or celery cabbage
1 cup bean sprouts
1 teaspoon herbal seasoning

BRANDY SAUCE

1 tablespoon reduced-sodium soy sauce	½ teaspoon honey
	½ jigger brandy
1½ teaspoons arrowroot or cornstarch	½ cup water

In a large skillet or a wok, heat the oil. Add the chicken pieces and cook until brown. Add the broth and remaining ingredients. Cover and cook for 15 minutes, then add the sauce.

TO MAKE THE SAUCE: In a small bowl, combine all the ingredients and mix until the sauce is thickened.

Yield: 4 servings.

Each serving provides: 218.5 cal, 15.7 g pro, 2.6 g sat fat, 8.3 g unsat fat, 66 mg chol, 241 mg sodium.

14
CHICKEN ON THE GRILL

Orange Teriyaki Chicken
Honey-Glazed Chicken Kabobs with Sesame, Onions, and Squash
Grilled Herb-Flavored Chicken Burgers
Grilled Chicken with Pine Nut or Walnut Pesto

To cook on a rack over hot coals, to invite the neighbors for a lovely picnic, to cause tantalizing aromas to invade the backyard, to obliterate all humdrum matters and stressful thoughts in anticipation of the joy of digging into a crisp-skinned, exquisitely flavored bird—that's grilling!

For the most delicious smoky flavor, start the barbecue about 40 minutes before you are ready to cook. The coals will then be grayed and burning at an even heat.

Recipes for broiled chicken can be grilled and vice versa. But bear in mind that charcoal broiling produces a higher direct heat, so cooking time will be shorter.

Marinades, commonly used on grilled chicken, contribute to a flavorsome moistness and tenderness. Marinades contain oil, an acid ingredient—vinegar or juice—for tenderizing, and seasonings for flavor.

When you grill kabobs over charcoal, place skewers on the barbecue rack, about 4 inches from coals, and turn the skewers frequently for even cooking.

To prevent dripping onto coals and causing flaming and smoking, remove the skewer from the barbecue grill when brushing it with marinade.

Orange Teriyaki Chicken

A spicy flavor zipped up with orange juice, which contributes valuable vitamin C, thus enhancing the utilization of the important minerals in all the ingredients.

¼ cup reduced-sodium soy
  sauce
3 tablespoons chopped onion
2 cloves garlic, minced
1 tablespoon olive or canola
  oil
½ teaspoon freshly ground
  pepper

½ teaspoon ground ginger
½ teaspoon Tabasco sauce
1 can (6-ounce) orange juice
  concentrate
2 broiler-fryers (2 to 2½
  pounds each), cut in
  serving pieces

In a bowl, combine all the ingredients except the chickens. Place the chicken pieces in a large bowl. Pour the orange juice marinade over the chicken. Marinate at least 3 hours, turning once, in the refrigerator.

Grill 4 to 6 inches from the heat source for 35 to 40 minutes, turning and basting with the marinade frequently.
Yield: 8 servings.
Each serving provides: 207 cal, 29 g pro, 1.5 g sat fat, 3.1 g unsat fat, 70 mg chol, 381 mg sodium.

Honey-Glazed Chicken Kabobs with Sesame, Onions, and Squash

Squash contributes calcium, magnesium, potassium, and vitamin A, all important to healthy bones and the glow of health. Onions have been shown to lower harmful cholesterol levels. Both add flavor and gusto to this dish, which hints of the Orient.

2 tablespoons sesame seeds, lightly toasted
¼ cup honey
¼ cup lemon juice
1 teaspoon herbal seasoning
¼ teaspoon Tabasco sauce
8 small white onions, peeled and lightly steamed
2 small yellow squash, cut in 1-inch slices and lightly steamed

1 large red pepper, cut into 2-inch pieces
1 large green pepper, cut into 2-inch pieces
8 chicken thighs
¼ cup oil and vinegar salad dressing

In a bowl, combine the sesame seeds, honey, lemon juice, herbal seasoning, and Tabasco sauce.

Using 4 long skewers, thread the chicken thighs with the squash, onions, and peppers. Brush with the salad dressing.

Barbecue 4 inches from the coals for 10 minutes, turning several times. Brush with the sesame seed glaze, turning and basting for 10 minutes longer.

Yield: 4 servings.

Each serving provides: 351 cal, 33 g pro, 2 g sat fat, 7.3 g unsat fat, 70 mg chol, 260 mg sodium.

Grilled Herb-Flavored Chicken Burgers

What's a cookout without burgers? Make yours with heart-healthy chicken. Enriched with oat bran and cornmeal, these burgers contribute valuable nutrients besides jolly enjoyment. Serve with sesame buns or whole wheat pita.

2 cups skinless, boneless
    chicken, cut in small
    cubes
¼ cup chicken soup or stock
1 teaspoon herbal seasoning
¼ teaspoon freshly ground
    pepper
2 tablespoons finely chopped
    fresh tarragon or 1
    teaspoon dried

½ cup cornmeal
½ cup oat bran
1 tablespoon chicken fat or
    olive oil
2 teaspoons lemon juice
2 tablespoons chopped parsley
¼ teaspoon Tabasco sauce
    (optional)

In a chopping bowl or food processor, grind the chicken coarsely. Add the soup or stock, herbal seasoning, pepper, tarragon, cornmeal, and oat bran. Mix to combine the ingredients; do not overmix. The mixture should not be pasty.

Divide the mixture evenly into 8 patties. Dampen your hands and shape the portions into round, flat patties. Chill thoroughly for at least an hour before cooking.

Preheat the grill to high. Brush the surface with a little oil or coat with a nonstick baking spray. Grill the patties for about 4 minutes. Turn and grill for another 4 minutes.

In a small skillet, heat the chicken fat or olive oil; add the lemon juice, parsley, and optional Tabasco sauce; and pour over the patties. Serve at once.

Yield: 8 patties.

Each patty provides: 124 cal, 11.4 g pro, 1 g sat fat, 6.3 g unsat fat, 66 mg chol, 64 mg sodium.

Grilled Chicken
with Pine Nut or Walnut Pesto

The combination of basil and garlic generates a marvelous appetite-stimulating fragrance. If you have any leftover sauce, use it to flavor fish, pasta, or salad dressing.

2 cups loosely packed basil leaves
⅓ cup olive oil
⅓ cup pine nuts or walnut pieces, lightly toasted

2 cloves garlic, peeled
1 teaspoon herbal seasoning
3 chicken breasts, skinned, boned, and split

TO MAKE THE PESTO SAUCE: In a food processor fitted with a metal blade, combine the basil leaves and olive oil, pine nuts or walnut pieces, and garlic. Process until smooth. Transfer to a small bowl.

Brush the chicken breasts all over with the pesto sauce. Grill the breasts over hot coals, brushing occasionally with more sauce until cooked through, about 6 minutes on each side.

Pass the remaining sauce at the table, or reserve for another use.

Yield: 6 servings.

Each serving provides: approximately 337 cal, 26.5 g pro, 2 g sat fat, 13 g unsat fat, 66 mg chol, 150 mg sodium.

15

LUSCIOUS, NUTRITIOUS STUFFINGS

Basic Bread Stuffing
Almond, Apple, and Bulgur Stuffing
Susie's Corn Bread Stuffing
Spicy Aromatic Rice Stuffing
David's Chestnut Stuffing
Kasha Stuffing with Mushrooms, Apples, and Raisins

Stuffings add an extra dimension of flavors, texture, and nutrients to the enjoyment of fowl. They can be made in infinite variety but tend to have a regional influence. In California they're into wild rice and mixed grains; in the Midwest stuffings are made with mushrooms, bread crumbs, and eggs; in New England they're usually made with chestnuts; and down South they're generally made with corn bread.

In the interests of food safety, many people opt to bake the stuffing as a casserole, where it develops a crisp crust.

If you prefer to put the stuffing in the bird, there are safety rules to heed.

According to the Turkey Talk-Line, the turkey, should be stuffed immediately before you put it in the oven, and the oven should be at least 350 degrees. The stuffing must be cooled before it is placed inside the bird and should be removed immediately after it is roasted. These measures retard spoilage.

Figure 1 cup of stuffing per pound of turkey.

A 13- to 15-pound turkey when stuffed should serve 24 people generously.

Pack the stuffing in with a light hand. Do not compress it, or it will be dense. Remember, it will expand during roasting.

Stuffings can be overly rich and outrageously caloric. They don't have to be. In the accompanying recipes I have reduced the fat, and with the addition of healthful grains and fruits enhanced the textures and flavors.

Basic Bread Stuffing

This is the traditional stuffing you probably remember so fondly, the way Mamma used to make it—but with a difference. This one is kind to your heart. The oat bran is a soluble fiber that lowers harmful cholesterol. The lecithin acts as an emulsifier that aids in the digestion of fats and breaks up cholesterol, helping to prevent atherosclerosis. The whole-grain bread and the wheat germ provide the B vitamins that fuel your energy pump and put a sparkle in your eye.

4 cups whole-grain bread cubes, lightly toasted
2 tablespoons poultry fat or olive, canola, or peanut oil
1 cup chopped onions
1 clove garlic, minced
1 cup chopped celery, including leaves
¼ cup wheat germ
¼ cup oat bran

2 tablespoons lecithin granules
½ teaspoon paprika
½ teaspoon ground sage
1 teaspoon freshly ground pepper
1 teaspoon dried thyme
2 eggs, beaten
½ cup chicken broth plus another ½ cup if stuffing is not cooked in bird

Place the bread cubes in a large bowl.

In a large skillet, heat the fat. Add the onions, garlic, and celery, and sauté until the onions are translucent. If it seems to need more fat, add a little chicken stock. Add this mixture to the bread cubes. Add the wheat germ, oat bran, lecithin granules, paprika, sage, pepper, thyme, and eggs. Toss. Add enough chicken broth to moisten the ingredients. Use to stuff poultry or add a little more broth, and bake in a greased baking dish at 325°F for 45 to 60 minutes or until lightly browned.

Yield: About 8 cups or 16 servings.

Each serving provides: 95 cal, 19 g pro, 0.5 g sat fat, 2.2 g unsat fat, 30 mg chol, 123 mg sodium.

Almond, Apple, and Bulgur Stuffing

A lovely combination of fruit, nuts, and grains. This makes a delicious casserole for a fish dinner when you don't have a bird to stuff.

2 tablespoons poultry fat or
    olive, canola, or peanut
    oil
1 large clove garlic, minced
1 cup chopped onions
1 cup chopped celery
4 cups poultry stock or water
1 cup bulgur
3 cups diced apples
½ cup chopped almonds
½ teaspoon ground nutmeg
¼ teaspoon allspice
½ teaspoon freshly ground
    pepper

In a medium-size saucepan, heat the fat or oil. Add the garlic, onions, and celery and sauté till the onions are wilted. Add the poultry stock or water. Stir in the bulgur. Bring to a boil, reduce the heat, then simmer, covered, for about 30 minutes.

Add the apples, almonds, and spices to the bulgur and mix well.

Yield: About 5 cups or 10 servings.

Each serving provides: 171 cal, 5 g pro, 0.7 g sat fat, 6.2 unsat fat, no chol, 31 mg sodium.

Susie's Corn Bread Stuffing

If you're from down South, you probably call it "dressing" and you wouldn't think of stuffing the bird with anything else.

3 tablespoons poultry fat or olive, canola, or peanut oil, or a combination
1 medium-size onion, chopped
1 large red bell pepper, chopped
2 ribs celery with leaves, chopped
¼ cup chopped parsley
2 scallions, chopped
6 cups 3-day-old corn bread, crumbled
1 cup oat bran crunch, crushed

½ cup wheat germ
2 tablespoons lecithin granules
⅓ cup chopped nuts (any kind, or a mixture of nuts and sunflower seeds)
1 tablespoon vegetable seasoning, or to taste
1 teaspoon freshly ground pepper
½ teaspoon sage
½ teaspoon Tabasco sauce
1 cup chicken broth if stuffing is baked in a casserole

In a large skillet, heat the fat or oil. Add the onion and sauté until it is wilted, about 5 minutes. Add the red bell pepper and celery and cook another 5 minutes.

Place the onion mixture in a large bowl. Add the parsley, scallions, corn bread, oat bran crunch, wheat germ, lecithin granules, nuts, vegetable seasoning, pepper, and sage. Stir to combine. When cool, fill the turkey with this mixture, being careful not to pack it. Leave room for expansion. Or, if you prefer, place the stuffing in a greased casserole and bake at 350°F for 40 minutes.

Yield: About 8 cups or 16 servings.
Each serving provides: 126 cal, 5 g pro, 0.4 g sat fat, 3.8 g unsat fat, no chol, 110 mg sodium.

Spicy Aromatic Rice Stuffing

Here's the intriguing flavor of the Orient enriched with brown rice, a good source of water-soluble rice bran, which, like oat bran, tends to lower harmful cholesterol levels.

2 cups chicken stock or water,
    or a combination
1 cup brown rice
2 tablespoons chicken fat or
    olive, canola, or peanut
    oil, or a combination
2 large onions, sliced
1 large garlic clove, minced
2 cups sliced mushrooms
½ cup raisins
2 teaspoons minced fresh
    ginger

¼ teaspoon ground cardamom
¼ teaspoon cinnamon
¼ teaspoon freshly ground
    pepper
⅛ teaspoon ground cloves
½ cup unsalted cashews,
    lightly roasted, coarsely
    chopped
1 cup chicken broth

In a medium saucepan, combine the stock or water and rice and bring to a boil. Reduce the heat, cover, and simmer until the rice is tender and the stock or water is absorbed—about 40 minutes.

    In a large skillet, heat the chicken fat or oil. Add the onions and garlic, cover, and cook, stirring occasionally, until the onions are translucent—about 8 minutes. Add the mushrooms, raisins, ginger, and spices, and cook for about 5 minutes, or until the mushrooms are soft. Remove from the heat. Stir in the cooked rice and the cashews.

Refrigerate before using.

Yield: About 7 cups or 14 servings.

Each serving provides: 96 cal, 3.5 g pro, 0.4 g sat fat, 2.8 g unsat fat, no chol, 42 mg sodium.

David's Chestnut Stuffing

Irresistibly good, the favored stuffing in New England—and a wise choice. Chestnuts bring a rich, nutty flavor, and yet they are very low in fat, only 1.5 grams per 100 grams as compared to almonds, which have 54 grams per 100 grams. The prunes are a flavorful counterpoint and provide lots of potassium, blood-building iron, and immunity-enhancing vitamin A.

1 pound chestnuts
2 cups pitted prunes
*   hot herbal tea to cover*
*   prunes*
1 turkey gizzard, trimmed of
*   tough membranes*
1 turkey liver
1 teaspoon poultry fat or
*   olive, canola, or peanut*
*   oil*
1 teaspoon ground sage
1 teaspoon rosemary

1 teaspoon herbal seasoning
½ teaspoon freshly ground
*   pepper*
2 pears, washed, cored, and
*   cut into small cubes*
3 apples, washed, cored, and
*   cut into small cubes*
½ cup coarsely chopped pecans
*   or walnuts, lightly*
*   toasted*
½ cup cognac

Unless the chestnuts are purchased already cooked, prepare them this way: With a sharp paring knife, make an incision around the perimeter of each chestnut. Place them in one layer in a baking dish. Bake in a preheated 450°F oven for 10 minutes or until they open. Let them cool until they can be handled, but peel them while they are hot. Cut them into ½-inch cubes.

Place the prunes in a bowl and add the tea to cover. Let soak until ready to use.

Grind together the gizzard and the liver. In a small skillet, heat the poultry fat or oil, and cook the liver mixture until it loses its raw, red color. Place this mixture into a bowl. Add the sage, rosemary, herbal seasoning, and pepper.

Drain the prunes and cut them into smallish pieces. Add them to the liver mixture. Add the chestnuts, pears, apples, nuts, and cognac. Blend well. Stuff a 10- to 12-pound turkey. Do not compress or pack the stuffing. If there is an excess of stuffing, place it in a small greased baking dish and bake along with the turkey for about 40 minutes.

Yield: About 8 cups or 16 servings.

Each serving provides: 132 cal, 3 g pro, tr sat fat, 2 g unsat fat, no chol, 15 mg sodium.

Kasha Stuffing with Mushrooms, Apples, and Raisins

Kasha or buckwheat is a warming food. Maybe that's why it's so popular in Russia. Kasha, which is roasted buckwheat, is high in fiber and a good source of rutin, a bioflavonoid, important to the building and maintenance of cartilage and an important antioxidant, a food factor that enhances your resistance to the development of carcinomas.

2 tablespoons poultry fat or olive, canola, or peanut oil
2½ cups chopped onions
2 cups sliced mushrooms
2 cups cooked kasha (cooked in chicken stock)
3 tart apples, washed, cored, and cut in small cubes

½ cup raisins
½ teaspoon cinnamon
1 tablespoon sage
1 teaspoon herbal seasoning
½ teaspoon freshly ground pepper
2 tablespoons lecithin granules

In a skillet, heat the poultry fat or oil and sauté the onions over moderate heat for 5 minutes or until the onions are translucent. Add the mushrooms, increase the heat slightly, and sauté the mixture for 3 minutes. Transfer to a large bowl and add the kasha, apples, raisins, sage, herbal seasoning, and pepper.

Yield: About 7 cups or 14 servings.

Each serving provides: 120 cal, 2.6 g pro, tr sat fat, 1.8 g unsat fat, no chol, 10 mg sodium.

16
LOVELY COMPANIONS

Cranberry Applesauce
Candied Sweet Potatoes
Potato Knishes
Sweet Potato, Apple, and Granola Bake
Noodle Kugel
Potato Kugel
Saffron Rice Salad
Broccoli with Shredded Wheat Topping

What you serve as side dishes with your chicken dinner provide the grace notes to a veritable symphony of flavors and textures. I like to serve something tart and moist, like a fruity dish, and something in the complex carbohydrate family, like rice, potatoes, or pasta. Such accompaniments not only complement the nutrients in the chicken, providing vitamin C and fiber, they also make for a very pleasant and enjoyable dining experience.

The recipes that follow provide a whole palette of colors, flavors, and textures to choose from.

Cranberry Applesauce

This sauce, made without any sweetener, is sweet enough to double as a jam, should you have any left over.

1 pound fresh cranberries
1 cup apple cider or apple juice
½ teaspoon cinnamon
9 small red apples, scrubbed, cored, and chopped
½ cup currants or raisins
1 tablespoon orange juice
2 teaspoons grated orange rind

Rinse and sort the cranberries.

In a large, heavy saucepan, bring the apple cider or apple juice to a boil. Add the cinnamon and cranberries. Boil until the cranberries begin to pop. Add the apples, currants or raisins, orange juice, and orange rind. Cover and simmer for 20 minutes. Purée the sauce in a blender or food processor if desired.

Yield: 7 cups or 14 servings.

Each ½-cup serving provides: 74 cal, no fat, no chol, 2 mg sodium.

Candied Sweet Potatoes

These have all the irresistible appeal of the usual candied sweet potatoes, but without added sweeteners. Each sweet potato provides as much as 11,610 units of beta-carotene, the nutrient that has been shown to retard the development of cancer. Sweet potatoes also provide potassium, calcium, and marvelous flavor.

> 6 good-size sweet potatoes
> 4 tablespoons fruit juice-
>   sweetened apricot
>   preserves or orange
>   marmalade

Bake or steam the sweet potatoes until soft. Split and place face up in a baking pan. Spread a teaspoon of preserves over each half. Place under the broiler for a few minutes, until the top is bubbly.
Yield: 12 servings.
Each serving provides: 85 cal, 1 g pro, no sat fat, 0.25 g unsat fat, no chol, 6 mg sodium.

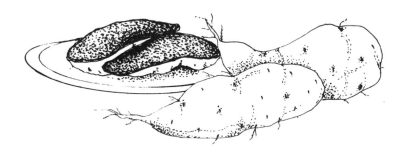

Potato Knishes

At our house, a supply of knishes in the freezer is better than money in the bank. They make any meal special and are a must for holiday meals. Our kids call these knishes "convertibles" because they don't have hard tops like knishes that are rolled in dough. These are much easier to make and very tasty. Potatoes are high in vitamin C complex, a better vitamin C pattern than is found in citrus fruit because it contains the tyrosinase fraction, an organic copper blood-builder. Potatoes also provide potassium, magnesium, calcium, and iron.

6 large potatoes, steamed in their jackets, then peeled and mashed
2 eggs, beaten (reserve 2 tablespoons)
grieben (chicken cracklings), as many as you can spare, chopped

1 onion, chopped and sautéed in 1 teaspoon chicken fat (if you don't have any grieben, sauté 2 chopped onions in 2 teaspoons chicken fat)
salt or vegetable seasoner and pepper to taste

In a large mixing bowl, mix together the mashed potatoes, beaten eggs, grieben and/or sautéed onions, and seasonings. Form into patties about ½-inch thick, 3 inches long, and 2 inches wide. Place on a cookie sheet coated with a no-fat cooking spray, or greased with a little chicken fat or oil. Brush the patties with the reserved egg. Bake in a preheated 375°F oven for about 35 minutes or until brown and fragrant.

Yield: 12 knishes.

Each knish provides: 60 cal, 2.5 g pro, tr sat fat, 1.2 g unsat fat, 41.6 mg chol, 10 mg sodium.

Sweet Potato, Apple, and Granola Bake

An excellent side dish and exceptionally nutritious. Apples provide a sweet tartness and gobs of pectin, which has been shown to decrease cholesterol concentration significantly, not only in the blood but also in the liver. In addition, pectin tends to bind with many toxic elements and ushers them out of the body. Granola is rich in morale-boosting vitamin B and valuable fiber.

4 *medium-size sweet potatoes*
   or yams
3 *medium-size apples*
1 *cup apple, orange, or*
   pineapple juice
1 *tablespoon arrowroot or*
   cornstarch

2 *tablespoons water*
1 *tablespoon honey*
½ *cup granola or wheat germ*
   chopped nuts (optional)
   cinnamon

Steam the sweet potatoes or yams for 15 to 20 minutes or until tender. Peel and cut in ½-inch slices. Layer in a 9×9-inch ungreased casserole. Wash and core the apples. Slice about ¼-inch thick and layer on top of the sweet potatoes or yams.

In a saucepan, heat the fruit juice to a boil. Combine the arrowroot or cornstarch and water and add it to the juice, cooking until the sauce has thickened. Add the honey and stir. Pour the sauce over the sliced apples, then top with granola or wheat germ. If using wheat germ, add some chopped nuts. Dust with a little cinnamon. Bake in a preheated 325°F oven for 30 to 40 minutes or until the apple slices are tender.
Yield: 8 servings.

Each serving provides: 127 cal, 1.7 g pro, tr sat fat, 0.5 g unsat fat, no chol, 5 mg sodium.

Noodle Kugel

Fantastic with chicken and so easy to prepare, this kugel is light as a soufflé and has a crunchy crust and a hearty flavor. Wheat germ and oat bran provide essential nutrients and fiber. Lecithin granules help keep cholesterol under control.

8 ounces fine noodles, cooked and drained	½ teaspoon freshly ground pepper
6 eggs, well beaten	¼ teaspoon cinnamon
2 tablespoons oat bran	2 tablespoons chicken fat or
½ cup wheat germ	olive, canola, or peanut
2 tablespoons lecithin granules	oil
2 teaspoons herbal seasoning	sesame seeds

In a large bowl combine the cooked noodles, oat bran, wheat germ, lecithin granules, herbal seasoning, pepper, and cinnamon. Mix well.

Heat 1 tablespoon of the chicken fat or oil in an 8 × 10-inch baking dish. Pour in the noodle mixture and top with sesame seeds. Drizzle the remaining chicken fat or oil on top. Bake in a preheated 400°F oven for 35 minutes or until nicely browned.

Yield: 10 servings.

Each serving provides: 180 cal, 8.6 g pro, 1.8 g sat fat, 5 g unsat fat, 150 mg chol, 42.4 mg sodium.

Potato Kugel

This crisp-crusted, moist, and savory kugel is a perfect partner for roast chicken or turkey and, in the food processor, can be made quick as a wink minus the scraped knuckles.

Potatoes are a good source of fiber, a good energy food, and low in calories. There are only 90 calories in a 5-ounce potato, which also provides 20 milligrams of vitamin C, as much as you would get in half a glass of tomato juice, as much protein as in half a cup of milk, and much more iron and niacin than in half a cup of milk. A real nutritional bargain.

3 large unpeeled potatoes, scrubbed and cut in 8 large dice
1 medium-size onion, cut in large dice
2 tablespoons wheat germ
2 tablespoons oat bran
2 tablespoons lecithin granules
1/8 teaspoon freshly ground pepper or to taste
2 teaspoons herbal seasoning, or to taste
dash of cinnamon
3 eggs
2 tablespoons chicken fat or olive, canola, or peanut oil

In a bowl or food processor fitted with a steel blade, whiz the potatoes and onions until well grated but not puréed. Add the wheat germ, oat bran, lecithin granules, herbal seasoning, pepper, cinnamon, and eggs. Whiz to combine.

Heat 1 tablespoon of chicken fat or oil in a 9 × 9-inch baking dish. Add the potato mixture. Drizzle the other tablespoon of chicken fat or oil over the top. Bake in a preheated 350°F oven for about 1 hour or until brown and crisp. Serve with applesauce.

Yield: 8 servings.

Each serving provides: 125 cal, 4.3 g pro, 1.4 g sat fat, 2 g unsat fat, 94 mg chol, 8 mg sodium.

Saffron Rice Salad

A warm-weather delight.

2 tablespoons wine or
    balsamic vinegar
1 teaspoon olive oil
1 clove garlic, minced
¼ teaspoon freshly ground
    pepper
2½ cups cooked brown rice,
    cooked in chicken broth,
    with ¹⁄₁₆ teaspoon saffron
    or ground turmeric

½ cup diced red pepper
¼ cup diced green pepper
¼ cup sliced green olives
¼ cup sliced ripe olives

In a large salad bowl, combine the wine or vinegar, olive oil, garlic, and pepper. Mix well. Add the rice, red and green peppers, onions, and olives. Toss to combine the ingredients.

Yield: 5 servings.

Each serving provides: 116 cal, 2.6 g pro, 0.1 g sat fat, 1 g unsat fat, no chol, 223 mg sodium.

Broccoli with Shredded Wheat Topping

Even your vegetable-scorners will go for this version. The crunchy topping contributes high-octane vitamin B's and lots of fiber. Broccoli, the darling of the vegetable bin, is a member of the cruciferous family, which has been shown to be an important ally in the fight against stomach and colon cancer.

1 bunch broccoli (about 1½ pounds), trimmed, cut in 1½-inch pieces, and steamed
1 teaspoon olive oil
⅓ cup chopped onion
1 clove garlic
½ cup crushed shredded wheat
½ teaspoon Worcestershire sauce

In a small skillet, heat the olive oil, add the onion and garlic, and sauté until golden, about 1 minute. Add the shredded wheat and Worcestershire sauce. Mix well. Place the cooked broccoli in a serving dish. Sprinkle with the shredded wheat topping. Place under the broiler for about 3 minutes, or in the microwave on high for 30 seconds.
Yield: 8 servings.
Each serving provides: 35 cal, 1.3 g pro, tr sat fat, 0.5 g unsat fat, no chol, 10 mg sodium.

INDEX

183

Ask for these titles at your local bookstore or order today.

Use this coupon or write to: Newmarket Press, 18 East 48th Street, New York, N.Y. 10017 (212) 832-3575.

Please send me:

Jane Kinderlehrer's SMART CHICKEN: *101 Tasty and Healthy Poultry Dishes, Plus Stuffings and Accompaniments*
———$12.95, paperback, 192 pages (ISBN 1-55704-073-7)
———$19.95, hardcover, 192 pages (ISBN 1-55704-100-8)

Jane Kinderlehrer's SMART BREAKFASTS: *101 Delicious, Healthy Ways to Start the Day*
———$11.95, paperback, 192 pages (ISBN 1-55704-045-1)

Jane Kinderlehrer's SMART COOKIES: *80 Recipes for Heavenly, Healthful Snacking*
———$11.95, paperback, 176 pages (ISBN 0-937858-62-5)

Jean Kinderlehrer's SMART MUFFINS: *83 Recipes for Heavenly Healthful Eating*
———$11.95, paperback, 176 pages (ISBN 0-937858-97-8)

Jane Kinderlehrer's THE SMART COOKIES/SMART MUFFINS GIFTSET
———$19.90, paperback shrinkwrapped giftset, two volumes: 352 pages (176 pages each volume) (ISBN 1-55704-052-4)

For postage and handling, add $2.00 for the first book, plus $1.00 for each additional book. Please allow 4–6 weeks for delivery. Prices and availability subject to change.

I enclose check or money order, payable to Newmarket Press, in the amount of $————.

Name————————————————————————
Address—————————————————————————
City/State/Zip—————————————————————

Clubs, firms, and other organizations may qualify for special discounts when ordering quantities of these titles. For more information, please call or write the Newmarket Special Sales Department at the above address.

KINDCHICK.5/91